No Safe Place

The Legacy of Family Violence

Christina Crawford

FOREWORD BY JOHN BRADSHAW

Station Hill Press

Published by Station Hill Press, Inc., Barrytown, New York, 12507.

Text and cover design by Susan Quasha,
assisted by Dominick Amarante and Vicki Hickman.

Front cover photograph by Vicki Hickman.
Back cover photograph by Bonnie Colodzin.

Library of Congress Cataloging-in-Publication Data

Crawford, Christina 1939-
  No Safe Place: The Legacy of Family Violence / Christina Crawford
    p. cm.
Includes bibliographical references (p.).
ISBN 0-88268-184-2: $12.95 paper
ISBN 0-88268-190-7: $24.95 cloth
  1. Family violence—United States—Psychological aspects. 2. Family violence—
United States—Case studies. 3. Victims of family violence—United States—
Psychology. 4. Victims of family violence—United States—Case studies. 5.
Crawford, Christina, 1939- . I. Title.
HQ809.3U5C73 1994
362.82'92—dc20
                               94-17737
                                  CIP

Manufactured in the United States of America.

No Safe Place

Books by Christina Crawford

Mommie Dearest

Black Widow

Survivor

No Safe Place

*This book is dedicated to my friends and fellow survivors
who have given me their stories and trusted me with their hearts,
hoping that we may all find a better life on this earth.*

Contents

Foreword

A few years ago, Christina Crawford and I appeared together on a TV show in Boston. Something very special happened that day. There was a kind of power in that program that can only come when two people talk from their hearts about a subject that they have both been the victims of. We talked about the many forms of family violence—abuse in all its ugly aspects, neglect, abandonment, and a child's enmeshment into their parents' unresolved conflicts.

I was amazed at the depth of Christina's clinical knowledge, but more impressed with the personal way that she expressed herself. I came to some deeper awareness about the problem of family violence by dialoguing with her that day.

No Safe Place: The Legacy of Family Violence embodies Christina's sharp insight into the roots of violence and how to stop it.

Many people believe that violence is about morally bad people—the thugs and hoodlums we see mugging and murdering people in the movies. Those stereotypes represent the fruits of violence, not its roots. Every murderer and mugger was once an innocent child who was willing to do anything to be loved by his parents. When they failed to get that love, they learned to confuse love with abuse.

When children are beaten for their own good, they numb out and can no longer feel the pain. The same thing happens in abandonment and neglect. If you can no longer feel the pain of your own abuse, abandonment, or neglect, then you can no longer feel the pain when you do it to your children. This is the tragic cycle of family violence. Pain causes numbing out and, when one is numbed out, he has no sense of pain when he inflicts it on others.

The most violent place in our country is the American family. If we could stop the violence in our homes, we could reduce the diagnostic book of psychiatric disorders to a pamphlet and empty three-fourths of our prisons.

We need a lot more than gun control and "three strikes you're out." We need to rethink motherhood, fatherhood, apple pie, and the American Way. This book does exactly that. It offers us a way of life that I like to call "deep democracy."

Christina Crawford talks from her heart. That is the place that violence can be healed. I know Christina has walked the walk and experienced everything that she writes about. I recommend this book with all my heart. It is one of the most important books that has crossed my desk in a long time.

John Bradshaw

Preface

As this book goes to press, media attention to the problem of violence in America and public concern about it seem to be mounting at a steady pace. We hear daily of ever-more virulent crime in the streets, shootings in school yards, gang violence among teenagers. Bizarre and hideous tales of the mistreatment of children by parents and caretakers are commonplace. We are deluged with reports of violence against wives by husbands, husbands by wives, unmarried women by lovers, minorities by legal authorities, incarcerated persons by incarcerating institutions. Serial killings are no longer once-in-a-decade events, and self-inflicted damage through addictions of every kind abound. Much of this violence is seen as "senseless" brutality, all the more terrifying because of its apparent lack of motive. But these crimes are very far from being uncaused, random occurrences: the causes are always there to be seen if we only have the courage to look at them. Present-day violence is caused by violence that began in the past in the homes and families of innocent victims who grew up to become its perpetrators. If violence is pervasive in the world of public events, it is because it is pervasive in our family lives.

Psychologists and students of society have long noted the connection between the traumas of childhood and the dysfunctional personalities of adults. But the fact that virtually every form of violence from which our society suffers can be traced to violence in the family is a devastating truth that has either gone unnoticed or been patently ignored. The well-nigh universal taboo against talking openly about the violence we have experienced in the sanctum of the family has prevented us as a society from seeing a blatant reality that is all but staring us in the face: violence in the world has its roots in violence in the home. If we ever hope to put an end to the brutality of our social environment, we will have to awaken, both individually and collectively, to the pervasiveness of what is happening at the very core of society.

Such an awakening would put us on the path of what we might call *social recovery*—a dedicated, collective commitment to change based on a clear-eyed diagnosis of the ills we wish to overcome, together with a determined and confident commitment to taking the steps necessary to overcome them.

No Safe Place not only offers such a picture of what is wrong, it provides a series of concrete proposals for change. It is with the hope that our society has the courage to step onto the path of social recovery by awakening to the "legacy of family violence," which lies beneath so many of our problems, that we have undertaken the publication of Ms. Crawford's latest work.

The Publishers

Ackowledgements

My gratitude to the following who have helped me bring this book to completion: Ben Colodzin, for his belief in my work and encouragement to continue it; Susan Ray, who helped transform this book through her editing; Carol Berreth, the angel without whom the manuscript would not have seen a word processor; Michael Brazzel, for his support through very tough times; Barbara Hayes, my true sister and joyful friend; Pam DuBois, whose persistent enthusiasm pushed me onward; the many dedicated professionals who have shared their courageous spirits with me; Vicki and Jim McNeill, who helped me find my way North; and Seven Springs Farm, my home, for daily gifts of beauty and sustenance.

No Safe Place

No Safe Place

No safe place.

Nowhere to hide. No way to escape the terror.

No one to tell. No one to go to for help.

Is this a war zone? A ghetto? A natural catastrophe?

No, this is the violence of day-to-day family life in many American homes. It is how I myself lived as a child, a teenager, and even as a young adult.

I did not grow up in a poor or blighted environment. I was a blonde, white child, my adoptive parent was a Hollywood movie star, and we lived in what many believed were luxurious surroundings. Still I carry deep and permanent scars from the violence of my childhood and developing years.

This was not violence from the outside world, from strangers or the streets, from gangs or muggers, but violence from those I, as a child, had been taught to love and trust, violence from those who were supposed to be safe and warm and filled with kindness but were not.

Fear followed me like an invisible shadow, for violence could erupt anywhere. It ambushed me in hallways, awoke me from sleep, disrupted the dinner table, spoiled my play in the backyard. Later, the continuing fear stole my friendships, denied me employment, and coerced and shamed me. More than any other event or person from my childhood, I remember the fear. It alone was constant; it alone could be counted upon. Whether awake or asleep, I was never free from its presence.

My adoptive mother was an angry, alcoholic woman who had clawed her way out of her own history of abuse and violence without ever healing or learning how to be a person along the way. She had no success establishing positive relationships with other adults that she couldn't manipulate and absolutely no idea what to do with children, except to control or punish them.

Perhaps she was simply passing along to others the only relationship sk. she knew.

Looking back on my life, I cannot recall when the fear started, because I have no memory of ever feeling safe or protected. My biological mother left me just after I was born. In the house where I was taken for adoption, I felt even less safe, for those people who were not actually violent towards me betrayed my confidence in order to please my mother or to stay employed by her. There was no safe place for me and not one soul I could trust.

Constant danger and betrayal created a life under siege. I never knew where the next disaster lay hidden, so every new circumstance held the threat of chaos. The least infraction of an extensive list of "rules of conduct" brought inappropriate, lengthy punishments, often lasting for months. Within this rigid, controlling atmosphere, I could not learn those skills acquired through trial-and-error because the risk of failure was too great. I learned only parental rules, how to imitate violence, and how to lie. To my amazement, lying—about anything—had less than a fifty-fifty chance of negative consequences, but telling the truth about my thoughts or feelings almost always resulted in violence or punishment.

I learned to withdraw into a tiny inner recess of self where nothing could enter. It wasn't the same as being safe from harm, but it was the only haven available to me. The self I showed to the world was no longer an authentic self, but one redesigned for the sole purpose of surviving violence on a day-to-day basis.

In time I began to perpetrate the violence I had experienced as victim against other children at school. By fourth grade I was engaging regularly in schoolyard fist fights, hurling swearwords I'd heard from adults at home, and lying even when there was no obvious reason to do so.

I was quite pretty and intellectually gifted, skipping grades in grammar school and eventually becoming the youngest student in my class. But I was also a highly emotional child, quick to anger, needing to have my own way, and slow to heal my wounds.

As a child, I learned from direct experience about violence in many forms, as physical punishment, abandonment, mistrust, shame, addiction, and betrayal. I did *not* learn how to value myself, how to form friendships, how to acquire new skills, how to resolve interpersonal conflict, how to evaluate strangers for trustworthiness, how to be kind to myself and others, how to accept help or assurance, or how to love and be loved.

What I did and did not learn as a child has affected the rest of my life. I spent my early years just trying to stay alive, while all the messages from without and within were telling me to give up and die. Eventually I shut

)andonment, terror, and helplessness. While I felt less
a terribly empty place in me which later, as a young
fill with cigarettes, alcohol, and sexual contact. It took
s and years of my adulthood to unlearn the lying, the
addic.   strust, and the abandonment of self and to learn the basic
skills of how .   e a person in the real world, how to earn a living, and how
to have a relationship that isn't destructive or violent.

What is violence?

Violence, according to *Webster's Dictionary*, is "an exertion of any physical
force so as to injure or abuse."[1] As I understand violence and will be using
the term in this book, it is the exertion of *any* force—whether physical, emotional, sexual, psychological, or spiritual—so as to injure or abuse.

Violence, now overwhelming our society, is by no means limited to criminal acts but is also employed as a primary means of conflict resolution, a
preferred form of play (e.g., video games), and a major factor in the content
and financial success of mass entertainment. Violence is also an orientation
toward sex, the nature and inevitable result of certain parenting behaviors,
the atmosphere in most urban schools, and the condition of life in almost any
American city. An acceptance of violence for fun and pleasure, violence
toward children and sexual partners, and the idea of violence as an unavoid-
able condition of human life has insidiously worked its way into our world
view and our understanding of how people relate to each other and create
their lives and environments.

The outcome, the implicit or explicit goal, of violence is death—death to
an opposing person or to an opposing quality or situation, such as resistance,
self-determination, or freedom. When violence wins, death of one kind or
another is the inevitable result. Violence threatens health, security, creativity,
kindness, and laughter—life in all its forms.

As violence takes over our society, the quality of our lives is declining. As
more money is spent for police, jails, and guns, there is less to invest in
essential, sustainable, healthy community projects. Violence has become an
organizing principle in the 1990s. We are at risk of losing ourselves in our
efforts to cope with violence, living only to react to its latest threat. Crisis
management has become our way of life.

What is family violence?

Family violence denotes actions taken by parents, caregivers, or other
family members that cause physical, emotional, or psychological trauma,
impair normal development, threaten personal safety, or create an atmosphere of danger. It includes but is not limited to child abuse, spousal bat-

tering and rape, murder, assault, enslavement, mental torture, kidnapping, stalking, addiction, and endangerment of health.

Family violence is *not* a one-time incident, and it is not a problem related to ethnicity, financial status, or gender. Nor is it a problem related only to drugs and crime, although these factors may be present in the violent home.

Family violence is the use—or misuse—of power over others who cannot defend themselves because they are smaller or weaker, who often cannot run away because they are too young to survive without parental care or too frightened of the violence they know they will have to endure if they are caught and returned home. Some will die because they cannot run away and others will die because they do.

In violent families, physical force is usually the primary means of asserting parental control, solving conflicts, and venting rage, anger, disappointment, and low self-esteem in the name of administering punishment.

Family violence can also take a sexual form, in which an older person makes sexual use of a child entrusted to their care without regard to the child's well-being. Such behavior involves emotional and/or physical coercion and probably is the result of some unresolved childhood trauma in the adult's past. Sexual violence is a violation of a young person's right to safety within the home, their right to say no, and their right to age-appropriate experience.

Emotional violence takes the form of shaming and humiliating behaviors by which, for example, a parent may attempt to feel better about him or herself by belittling the child in the hope of at least feeling superior to *someone.*

Members of violent families learn that violence always wins, at least in the short term: the violent always get their way. After a while, they get their way whether they behave in an overtly violent manner or not.

Witnessing violence toward others and feeling powerless to intervene extracts a toll on all family members involved. At the very least, it desensitizes them and creates co-conspirators, insuring that no one feels totally blameless—except perhaps the perpetrator.

It is like the story about the frog and the pot of boiling water. If a frog is thrown into a pot of hot water, so the story goes, it will immediately try to jump out. However, if that same frog is put into a pot of lukewarm water and the heat is turned up gradually, the frog will stay in the pot until it is boiled to death.

In my experience, trying to avoid the violence while remaining in the family household doesn't work. It's like staying in the pot of water until you die. The violence will occur over and over again.

Violence is addictive. The violent person becomes addicted to the power and the thrill of using violence against others, particularly when the chance of getting hurt him or herself is almost nonexistent. Violence stimulates adrenalin, so with it, there's a "rush," just as with many drugs that the addict experiences as pleasurable. And as with other addictions, the addiction to violence grows progressively worse over time, and the addict is almost never able or willing to stop violent behavior without outside intervention. He or she may have been brought up with violence, and no one ever said *his or her* parents were wrong.

At some point, the mere threat of violence can replace the actually violent acts, for the threat alone evokes vivid memories of past violence under similar conditions. The victims are duped or brainwashed into believing that they actually allowed or participated in their own punishment and begin to feel both guilt and shame that they can do nothing to stop the violence against others in the family. Everyone is justifiably afraid of the violent person, and so they regulate all behavior to avoid as much hurt as possible. Violence thus becomes the "norm" for day-to-day existence. After a while, if nothing happens to attract outside attention or help, the family members sink into an angry, depressed state of resignation.

When we were both small children, I was forced to watch my brother being beaten, humiliated, and burned. Just three years younger than I, my brother soon changed from a charming and adorably playful little boy into an angry runaway. I spent the next thirty years trying to make it up to him, while enraged at the woman who vented her hatred of men on an innocent little boy.

Why is it so important to understand family violence?

It is important to understand it because of its legacy, because family violence has directly or indirectly left its black mark on almost every aspect of our world civilization.

We live in an incredibly complex and highly interconnected society, where any violence cannot help but impact everyone. Even small amounts of violence create large amounts of havoc and social disruption. Family violence inevitably spills out onto the streets and into the next generation in some form or another. Billions of taxpayer dollars are poured into institutions such as foster care, hospital emergency rooms, prisons, police, social services, courts, etc. to deal with violence *after the fact.*

This money is not used to *prevent* violence. It is not spent on treating addictions, improving schools, teachers, transportation, child day care, neighborhoods, or jobs. There simply isn't enough time, energy, or money to address more positive approaches and long-range planning when daily life has become a matter of crisis management.

Many thousands, perhaps millions, of young people are showing signs of becoming sociopathic, of lacking conscience and empathy for others, of feeling no bond to family or responsibility to community. Many of these young people, barely more than children, have never been properly parented. They have no sense of having been respected or nurtured by those responsible for them as children. And because they lack this sense of respect, safety, and nurturance in themselves, they cannot possibly offer it to their children.

In the past, it has been assumed that once the violence stopped, its effects also stopped. That assumption is dangerously untrue. It has prevented us from seeing that *violence is a lifestyle, not an isolated incident.*

Family violence has been called *domestic* violence for many years—a serious misnomer, one that has contributed to our reticence in addressing its horrors and dangerous consequences.

Domestic refers to that which has been tamed or modified for ordinary household or community usefulness. It is not a word appropriate to the terror and chaos of violence in the home. *Household terrorism* would be a far more accurate term.

Our legal system has a completely different set of laws for those crimes committed on the streets, against total strangers, than it has for those same criminal behaviors committed in the home against family members. All manner of crime, including murder, is often not counted as "real" crime if it is committed in the home against a spouse, child, or other blood relative. Such acts fall into the category of *domestic dispute*; in the past, no one wanted to deal with them. Neither police nor social service workers wanted to answer the call for fear of being hurt themselves in a situation so explosive and so ambivalent in terms of legal protection. Our society has permitted family members to be treated with more violence and less protection than is accorded prisoners of war under the terms of the Geneva Convention.

Such an attitude leaves victims/survivors of family violence on their own to deal with the damages done them. Not only are they without support and encouragement from others, they are often blamed for what happened to them and shamed for the fears and defenses they carry as a result. As in childhood, telling the truth carries negative consequences for them. If they speak, family members will likely become distant or alienated, and the social and legal power structures created supposedly to help just such victims of injustice frequently dismiss them with no questions asked.

What are the effects of family violence on its victims/survivors?

Many would (and do) prefer to forget the horrible past and just try to get on with their present lives. Others tend to get stuck, blaming every setback and failure on the past. In the process of healing the emptiness and the anger, some others become activists engaged in changing social systems and behavior patterns, in creating social awareness, and in educating others from their own experience. Millions more live life on the outermost edges of our world, as survivalists or the homeless, who are marginalized into near oblivion. Many folks simply do not make it: they are institutionalized, they commit suicide, they are murdered.

Yet, as the exceptions that are said to prove the rule, others survive, succeed, and thrive. Perhaps that is the miracle of humanity: against all odds, some will always manage to achieve a state of relative healthiness in order for the species to evolve. However, if over time too many people are incapacitated, made unable to cope and thrive by prolonged childhood violence with its fundamental disrespect for human life, a dangerous downhill slide in the quality of our society will take over and threaten life as we know it.

When violence becomes the norm in a family, its members have to dedicate most of their energy, thought, and time to survival, rather than to growth and development. They develop a sort of violence-oriented ESP, an early warning system that provides split-second notice for self-protection. I believe survivors make excellent detectives, investigators, spies, and psychologists, for their intuitive senses are finely attuned to others' behavior and to interpreting what that behavior means. Often survivors choose to go into one of the helping professions (law, education, medicine, healing) in order to help others with the same problems and, in so doing, right some of the wrongs they experienced.

But survival behavior is very different from the developmental processes of those who have not experienced abuse and violence as children. For example, survivors tend to isolate themselves, drawing only on their own strengths, intelligence, information gathering skills, and intuition. Since the outside world has proven to be very dangerous and unpredictable, it is safer not to interact, trust, depend, or count on anyone other than oneself. Such behavior denies the survivor the experience of caring and being cared for that is the foundation of all social interaction, coupling, and parenting.

Survival behavior is usually a poor basis for healthy adult relationships, and since relationships are what create community, workplace, couples, and family, having *only* survival skills puts a person at a serious disadvantage—until or unless they return to a violent, disrespectful relationship, in which at least they can feel "at home." Violence, by this means as well as others, tends to perpetuate itself. Have you ever wondered why someone you know stays in a harmful relationship or situation? The answer is: they know how it works!

Adult survivors of family violence experienced in childhood often manifest a high tolerance for violence in their partners or spouses. They themselves may use violence against others. Adults who have experienced violence in childhood have learned the raging tone of voice, the threatening looks, the swift and dangerous fist or foot. They know the pattern, the process, and the result: with violence you get what you want, no matter the cost to others— survival of the fittest. It is very hard for the adult survivor to comprehend that imitation of parental behavior is no compliment, but a crime against the next generation of children and society at large. But the legacy of violence against others as a means to self-fulfillment is very powerful.

Other victims/survivors of family violence will not permit any overtly violent acts by others or themselves, but they still may engage in self-destructive behaviors (not taking care of themselves, becoming addicted, creating conditions of chaos, etc.) that may not be fully conscious.

Ironically, it may be this very legacy of violence, this collection of fears and behaviors learned so long ago and so early in life that discourages those of us who survived family violence from confronting the issue in our society today.

I believe the reluctance comes from real fear, fear born in the childhood experience of retribution for exposing the truth. As adults, such retribution from others perceived as being more powerful than we are may take the form of professional retaliation, being ostracized, or having our ideas denigrated. These possibilities are so similar to what actually happened to us as children raised in violence that the current situation may feel like a replay of the past— of being powerless, disbelieved, and unable to defend oneselves or to escape from the problem. Those of us raised in an atmosphere of family violence learned early in life that the world is an unsafe place. As adults, we may still base our beliefs and actions on that world view, however hidden we keep it from everyday consciousness.

The configuration of violence, resignation, and negative learning in the survivor is currently supported by an abundance of extremely violent movies and books, super-hero role models, violent cartoons, news of violence on TV, callous handgun/assault weapon laws, and a social structure that devalues children, women, the weak, and the aged, as well as the professions of teaching, caregiving, and nurturing.

After all the years of disclosure, media attention, social service expenditures, and public awareness programs about child abuse and family violence, almost nothing has been accomplished to solve the problem. Reputable research indicates that violence and abusive behavior have *increased* across social strata.[2] It is likely that an entirely different approach to the problem must be taken in order for substantial change to be affected. With this book, I hope to offer a perspective that will help in the formulation of that new approach, that new organizing principle.

I offer my own life journey as an example, one among millions of stories of survivors of family violence. My story makes the point, raised earlier, that family violence is addictive, and that the incidents of violence are not isolated, but rather form the basis of family relationships.

But my intention here is not just to rehash the details of years of abuse all over again. I wrote my first book, *Mommie Dearest*, in the only way I could have written it, for myself, with no other goal than to tell what really happened and set the record straight. I had no idea anyone outside my immediate family would read it. I had no idea it would be published.

That book was written from the point-of-view of a child in the process of growing up. This book is written from the perspective of years of adult learning and experience attained in the process of healing my life.

If *Mommie Dearest* was written from a sense of outrage and injustice, *No Safe Place* is written from the need to share information and insight and to honor those who have shared with me their life stories, in letters and personal contact, so that a solution can be found to the tragic problem of family violence. *No Safe Place* is generated from the knowledge that if violence within the family is not addressed, we as a society will never be able to stop the violence on the streets, between races, nations, and religions, which creates the feeling that there is no safe place for anyone, anywhere, anytime.

The Legacy
of
Family Violence

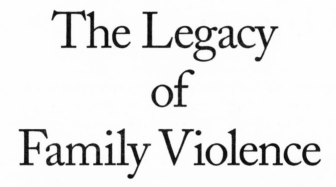

CHAPTER 1

The Legacy of Family Violence

Many children learn quickly that they can get their personal needs for love and care met by their parents. Thus bonds are formed, trust is created, and protection and guidance are offered until the small people can manage in the world by themselves.

This was not my personal experience of early life.

My body was physically hurt, punished, and ridiculed. My mind was programmed for servitude and made susceptible to manipulation. I was never allowed to express a choice freely or say no. My spirit was humiliated, terrorized, and prohibited from spontaneously embracing life, health, and happiness.

Instead of being protected, guided, and loved, I was taught to be ashamed, alone, frightened, suspicious, enraged, and empty, that I didn't belong anywhere and that nothing belonged to me. If anyone in the house expressed particular affection for me, they were dismissed. If I showed special preference for a friend or a toy, it was taken away from me. I was not permitted to lock bathroom doors or to keep a private diary. There was no *mine* or separate *me*. I was intended only as an appendage to my adoptive mother. I survived at her pleasure and could easily be destroyed the same way. That particular lesson I learned very early.

As a small child, I was hit and beaten with objects, threatened, deprived of basic necessities such as food and sleep, ignored, abandoned, disrespected, sexualized, and manipulated. I was told that I was a "selfish girl, ungrateful, not to be trusted, and a bad influence" on my siblings. I was constantly in trouble, living out the misery of childhood on a second chance basis, convinced that I was a fundamentally flawed human being and that probably nothing would ever set me right.

I felt terror of my mother's erratic, totally unpredictable behavior toward me and others. No matter what I did or how hard I tried, there was never any truce, peace, or safety. Fear of her next outbreak was everpresent. Yet I needed her. I was a child and I could not take care of myself. I didn't know the difference between real love and dependence. I believed that because I needed and depended on her for survival, I should also love her. The fact that in my secret heart I did not have those feelings was very confusing.

Recently, after I spoke at a women's conference, a woman introduced herself as having been a classmate of mine in fourth grade. She recounted an incident I'd long forgotten, but which had etched itself in her memory. Evidently I had brought a photo of my adoptive mother to school, probably because a classmate had requested it. When asked about it, I held out the picture and said flatly, "I hate my mother." This statement from an eight-year-old astonished my old school friend even then.

Until sixth grade, I went to public school and lived at home. During those years (1943-1950), my mother was struggling with her third stormy marriage and having major problems with her career.

Sometimes she would demand that all the other people in the house—the cook, secretary, gardener, and cleaning woman—not speak to me. Days would go by and no one except the governess would look at me or direct a single word my way. Other times she would try to make them treat me like a "bad girl," using unkind looks or a degrading tone of voice.

At night, from my bed, I would hear arguments, swearing, screaming, door slamming, and the resounding crash of thrown objects. In the dark I would pray that nobody remembered I was alive in the next room. I lay so still my body became stiff, as though frozen or dead. Sometimes I didn't dare breathe for fear someone would hear, as unlikely as that was, given all the other noise.

I would hear footsteps and the sounds of people running up or down the stairs. Sometimes dark figures would run right through my room out onto a balcony, where the fight continued. Still frozen with terror, I would pretend to be asleep. No matter how much I wanted to pull the covers over my head for protection, I dared not move a muscle. Later my mother would comment, "You sleep so soundly, a circus could go through your room and you'd never hear it."

When I was about ten years old and watching television in another room, I heard the sound of my mother being hit by a man. I ran to help her. I started punching the man, kicking at him and yelling. He left quickly. She allowed herself to be helped upstairs. A week or so later, the man was back, and, to my horror, I was forced to apologize to him for my intrusion and "bad manners."

Today I recognize that early message as very similar to the one we receive as a society: Do not interfere. Turn your back and go on about your own business.

Until I was sent to boarding school and lived away from home most of the time, I was forced to watch while my little brother was beaten. We shared a room and we tried to help each other whenever we could, secretly, without anyone else seeing. During those horrible times when he was being hurt, I was also scared for myself and enraged with my mother. I felt absolutely powerless to help him and prayed only for the strength to live through that day or night.

My physical punishments from the age of four to sixteen took many different forms. I was beaten, slapped repeatedly in the face, tied up and left in the shower, locked up and left in a dark closet, denied food for days at a time, deprived of sleep, and prevented from seeing friends or receiving phone calls and letters. When I was asked by the woman who took care of us how I ended up tied in the shower, I told her I didn't know. To this day, I still do not know; the memory has never returned.

Once I was playing on the swings with a girlfriend when suddenly I saw a lot of blood staining my underpants. I was only about seven or eight years old, so it was not the onset of my menstrual period. The sight of blood, particularly my own, upset me, so by the time I had run up to the house to get help, I was nearly hysterical. My vagina was cut and bleeding profusely, but no one called for the doctor or took me for medical treatment. I was washed off and told to lie down in bed until the bleeding stopped. Then I was not supposed to play in the yard, swing on the swings, or walk up and down the stairs for a week or more. Various people carried me upstairs for a while, and nothing more was said. The official explanation was that I had hurt myself on the swing, but my underpants were not torn and I hadn't been playing very hard. And no one seemed upset besides me.

Life as a child was mysterious. Things happened for which there was no sensible explanation. People left without saying goodbye. Nobody knew where they were going, whether or not they were ever coming back, or what had happened to cause them to go.

I was programmed mentally and emotionally to expect and endure violence, cruelty, and intentional harm. Violence stripped me of trust and innocence. It does that to every child it touches. All my energy was used to cope with the violence. There was little time left with which to learn the skills and behaviors needed for successful adulthood.

If I made friends at school, my mother tried to co-opt them. If that didn't work, she would manipulate them into taking sides with her against me or create a horrible scene when they came over to play so that they would be sure never to return. This pattern of behavior continued through my fresh-

man year in college, when I finally learned to keep
precious to me away from her. She still managed, howe
job I ever had, acting on a soap opera, and to try to keep
with any of her friends in Hollywood during my years as   ...y,
I gave up fighting such an uphill battle. I left the entertain   ... ousiness and
returned to college. After obtaining my master's degree, I began a career in
communications that kept me out of her grasp and brought me some success.
Even after all the years that have passed, I can't help wondering what I might
have been able to make of my life if pain and chaos had not claimed so much
of my thought, time, and energy.

It wasn't until about five years ago that I realized how deeply the violence
of my childhood had permeated the whole of my life. It was the first time that
anyone said out loud to me that my fear of my mother and of the house in
which I lived as a child was not usual. My therapist told me that home for
a child is supposed to feel safe, protected, and secure.

My first feelings of safety, after forty years of living in fear, did not come
from alarm systems, locks, guns, or guard dogs—although I had those, too.
I won a feeling of safety against the constant anxiety and fear only when the
terrors and demons of my childhood had been reckoned with enough that
they no longer governed my reactions to every moment of every day. I began
to feel safe when I began to feel worthwhile as a woman and connected to
my community as an adult. Only then could my body begin to unfreeze, to
uncurl itself from the fetal position in which I slept each night as the only
protection I felt I had left. Only then could I sleep more than a few hours at
a time without suffering terrifying nightmares that left me exhausted and
lying in a pool of sweat and tears.

In my late teens and early twenties, when I felt most despondent and
helpless, I would daydream about going to my adoptive parent's funeral. I
would see her lying dead in her coffin and myself standing beside her body
for a long time to make sure that there were no signs of life, that death was
not a trick, that she would not suddenly arise and laugh derisively at the
deception. Then I would see myself standing at the gravesite and watching
the coffin being covered with dirt. Everyone else was crying, while I was
thanking God for being merciful and ridding the world of an evil force that
destroyed everything it touched.

It still amazes me that I didn't suffer a total nervous breakdown or act out my
daydream in real life. I certainly felt the rage. Sometimes, sad to say, I still do.

When *Mommie Dearest* was published in 1978, some hailed it as a work of courage, as a breakthrough in our society's wall of denial about child abuse.

Others recoiled from its truth, terrified of breaking the taboo against speaking ill of parents. Still others found it hard to understand because their own lives had not, as yet, been touched by violence.

And some people realized that their own experience of violence, their family nightmare, their lonely terror at home was real. With this validation, they, too, found a voice. They, too, could use that voice to speak up for themselves, to speak out against what had happened to them, to demand that the violence against themselves and other innocent people come to a halt. The book took on a life of its own and became a catalyst for social change, helping to transform not only interpersonal behavior, but also those larger social and legal institutions that mediate reforms.

But the social consequences of truth-telling can take many forms, some of them harsh, including ostracism, ridicule, accusations of lying, organized backlash to protect the powerful, threats of damnation, family hostility, and even loss of work and blacklisting. I myself experienced many of these after the publication of *Mommie Dearest*. And, of course, none of those consequences are what we are prepared for when adults speak to us as children of the virtues of telling the truth.

As this truth-and-consequences drama was playing itself out in the public arena, letters poured in from all over the country reporting monumentally horrible childhood histories made worse because no one had helped their survivors or believed them when they sought help. They poured out their secrets and hearts to me, saying that for the first time they felt their experience validated and they no longer felt alone and crazy.

In the midst of my own crisis of trying to cope with the frenzied response to my book and the misrepresentations about me, the book, my intentions, and my veracity, those letters gave me courage. They were specific and instructive. They taught me to look beyond the immediate miseries of a violent childhood and to begin to see the long-term damage, which had not yet been acknowledged. Some of these letters were written from prisons and hospitals. All gave me information about the range of abusive behaviors, their emotional intensity and duration. I was amazed at the human child's capacity to survive such cruelty. It was clear, however, that the cost of such survival was very high.

Gradually, from what I read in the letters together with what I knew from my own experience, some patterns began to emerge:

1. The abusive parental (or caretaker) behavior did not stop until the child/victim/survivor left the home or died. However, the psychological abuse, administered verbally, continued even at a distance.

2. There were others besides the parent and child (i.e., other abusers and/or other victims) involved.

3. No one protected or rescued the child, though the abuse was never a complete secret.

4. Most people felt that their parents did not want them or love them and blamed them for life's misery.

5. No external consequences were incurred by the abusing parent.

6. Many felt their parents were "possessed" when they behaved violently, even when drugs or alcohol were not present.

7. Many survivors described a split personality in their parents, one personality for the outside world and a very different one inside the home.

8. Many victims/survivors did not understand the life-long consequences of the abuse and continue to live in confused desperation as adults.

9. Most survivors reported multiple problems in adult life, such as addictions, mental health issues, migraine headaches, chronic pain, and difficult relationships with friends and partners.

10. The saddest stories were of survivors trying to get help and being re-abused and re-victimized by professionals in medicine, law, religion, social services, and metaphysics.

It is clear to me now that we survivors often relive as adults our nightmarish childhood experiences. The violence of these relived experiences came close to killing me many times during the fifty and more years of my life.

The onset of adulthood for me, and for millions like me who were on their own in their teens without benefit of a real childhood, was one step forward, three backwards; marking time, not making progress; constantly making mistakes that I didn't even know were mistakes, so I couldn't do better next time; feeling as though I did not belong anywhere, except perhaps with a group of others who were similarly disadvantaged; not knowing how to ask for help and fearing that asking would give others ammunition against me; not taking very good care of myself, but being very concerned with my appearance.

No one had ever taught me how to care for or respect myself. Closeness with an adult meant either sex or violence or both. Because no one had had compassion for me or my needs, I didn't know what compassion toward others might feel like. Without compassion, there was no empathy or real contact with others, and so no sense of us all being joined together in this world. Without compassion, I felt alone and angry.

In order to stay alive in that unlivable reality, at a very young age I learned the technique of *numbing,* a technique used commonly by children living in traumatic circumstances. I retreated to an alternate reality, a world of imagination, a world without pain. This alternate reality had both constructive and destructive aspects to it. While it was a brave attempt to create balance and safety out of chaos, it also could have become life-threatening by evolving into psychosis and multiple personality, and it was highly vulnerable to failure. But whether this world of imagination was primarily a positive or negative force, I had to keep it a secret or risk being labeled crazy.

Abused children learn to keep two worlds a secret: the real world of terror and violence from which they are trying to flee and the imaginary world of safety to which they escape for comfort. In order to manage everyday life, they construct a third world behind which to hide the other two.

A giant myth has been perpetrated that children forget or fantasize (i.e., make up) the abusive parental behavior they suffered or claim to have suffered, and that violence experienced in childhood has no lasting negative consequences. This myth is believed and supported by such diverse groups as Freudian psychoanalysts, the media, government, the courts, fundamentalist sects, and vast segments of the general public, none of whom want to know differently.

Children cannot make up behavior for which they have no previous language, image, or frame of reference. On the other hand, "forgetting" or burying the brutal experiences of childhood for periods of time is not at all uncommon when the experiences were perceived by the child as life-threatening, when the trauma was of such magnitude that remembering it is literally unbearable and comparable to dying.

Adults are sometimes viewed as springing forth from puberty, as chickens hatch out of eggs, carrying no trace of their childhoods; but the experiences of childhood are, along with genetic make-up, the major influences on the development of an adult.

For most adults who have experienced childhood trauma, life continues chaotically until a serious crisis hits. Then the entire house of cards built of defenses, lies, and charades comes tumbling down. At that point, these people either go for help or give up.

One evening, when I was home from boarding school for a rare weekend visit, my mother took me out to dinner with some of her friends. She'd been drinking. She told her friends I had been expelled from school. It was a total fabrication. I was a model student, on the honor role, a cheerleader, an athlete.

At home, I protested. She slapped me so hard it made my ears ring. "You just love to make me hit you, don't you?" she said. I was thirteen years old. We were nearly the same height.

As she did not want anyone else to hear more of our dispute, she called me into the bar area. There she hit me again, throwing me off balance. I fell to the floor, hitting the back of my head on an ice chest. She climbed on top of me and began to choke me, banging my head on the floor. I thought she was trying to kill me.

After someone separated us, I was taken upstairs and locked in a back bedroom. The juvenile authorities came, and the officer told me she had called them and asked them to take me away, declaring me "incorrigible."

Something inside me snapped. That night I understood that the world is an insane place. What else can you call it? A society that permits parents to attempt murder and then tries to lock up the *victim* has to be crazy.

The officer did not take me to juvenile hall that night. He advised me to try to get along until I was eighteen and could go out on my own, because there was no other help for me.

Those who have not lived through serious trauma during childhood and whose early years were relatively normal see the world differently from those of us who are survivors. When they refer to *mother*, *father*, and *family*, they have in mind images very different from mine for exactly the same words.

I am now convinced that this *one* element of difference is responsible for a vast chasm of misunderstanding which, at least until now, has been exceedingly difficult to cross. I am equally convinced that we have never quite come to terms with this underlying misunderstanding that makes it so hard to discuss mother-father-family violence without creating more fear and greater misunderstanding.

No one from my family attended my high school graduation. I spent the following summer alone at boarding school. In the fall, I took a train to college in Pittsburgh, Pennsylvania.

After a year at Carnegie Mellon University as a drama major, I went to work in summer stock at a theater in Connecticut and then on to New York City. I attended professional school for the next year. At nineteen years old, I was on my own. I worked as a cashier in an Italian restaurant for $10 and a meal a night, while looking for acting work during the day. A year later I acted in a film, some commercials, more summer stock, and finally I landed a long-term contract in Hollywood with 20th Century Fox Studios. My first part was in a picture with Elvis Presley.

After the film was finished, my contract was cancelled, for my mother had called the producer and told him that she would not work on the same studio lot with me. His next picture was to feature her in a cameo. He could hardly look at me as he mumbled how sorry he was and wished me luck.

Six months later, unable to find enough acting work to sustain myself, I took a full-time job in the mailroom of a savings and loan in Hollywood. It paid fifty dollars a week. I stayed there two years while I tried to figure out what to do with my life. In a way, those were peaceful years. I had broken off all contact with my mother and, since I was no longer in show business and she neither called nor wrote, it was a real respite.

Through an odd series of events, friends from my New York days found me and got me summer acting jobs in midwestern theaters. Then I auditioned for the road company of *Barefoot in the Park* and got the part. I was soon on my way to Chicago to rehearse.

It was there that I met my first husband, who was directing the replacement actors. While my reviews were great and I received a critics' award for my performance, the star of the show took a dislike to me and insisted that I be replaced. It was chaos again.

The director and I were married. Mother insisted on arranging the wedding. I went to live in New York once again and resumed my relationship with her, this time as a "favored" child.

Less than a year later, my marriage was falling apart. I was twenty-seven years old. I decided to seek psychological help. It was clear to me that there was a basic flaw in my ability to relate to others, but how to fix it escaped me entirely. All I knew was that I felt angry all the time. I could not negotiate disagreements. Arguments felt like betrayal. I felt abandoned every time my husband left town for work, which was often.

After months of private therapy sessions made extremely painful by my lack of trust, I reluctantly agreed to join a therapy group.

I endured the group sessions in near silence for several months. Slowly, I began to be able to hear the others as they shared their secrets and fears. Since I saw everyone every week, I became somewhat assured that one did not die from these disclosures. In fact, the others seemed to make progress, to be accepted, to actually enjoy the companionship of the other group members.

With great caution, I spoke a few sentences, tentatively joined a discussion, began to interact a little. After about a year, I looked forward to the meetings and felt friendship toward some group members. This experience of being real, of being myself, *and* of being accepted as myself was totally new and pleasurable for me. My marriage, however, did not improve.

One afternoon, in a moment of rare candor at a group session, I remarked that I needed to free myself from the hold that my relationship with my mother had on my life, because no matter how much progress I made in therapy, no matter how much my attitude toward myself changed, our relationship did not change for the better. It still felt destructive and thwarting.

The therapist replied that I would never be free of my mother—at least, that is what I think I heard her say. I realized by her look that she meant no malice, but her words came at me like a bullet from a gun, almost knocking me backwards in my chair. I could not hear another word spoken, by her or anyone else in the room. My trust, fragile as it had been, was shattered.

I bolted out of my chair screaming, "Why the hell am I here then? What the hell am I paying all this money for? You're condemning me to live in hell for the rest of my life!"

What I couldn't say was that if I did not free myself, I would die from the pain of being half-dead and half-alive all the time. If there was no way out, no hope of a life with less pain than this, then there was no sense to the struggle; the effort I was making day after day was pointless. My tears fell uncontrollably. I could barely breathe. Everyone stared at me, shocked. I felt like an animal trapped and caged.

What I had just heard reflected was a point of view, an organizing principle diametrically opposed to the one I needed to hold to in order to stay alive. According to that point of view, the parent is right, the child is wrong; the parent has the power, the child has none; the wishes of the parent are the rule, the needs of the child are inconsequential. Opposition, expression of one's separate being, affirmation of one's rights are not acceptable.

What I needed was information on a new way for me to be in the world. What I wanted was freedom from the invisible, lethal entanglement by which I was defined only by my relationship to my mother, not as a person in my own right. In that light, what I heard from the therapist sounded like a death sentence.

I already knew that no amount of progress on my part was going to change the relationship between my mother and myself at its foundation. (Ten years later, that intuitive knowledge was confirmed. After all the work on my part, she left a will disinheriting me "for reasons well known" — except there was no explanation. When my brother and I contested the will, we learned that the disinheritance clause had been brought forward intact from wills written as many as twenty years before.)

Discovering and nurturing my own authentic self was my sole salvation, a life and death issue, because I could not continue living with such a bruised and trapped spirit, nor did I want to. The way I saw it, I had no choice but to flee—from the room and from the therapist's way of thinking— in order to save my own life. Sheer adrenalin propelled me into the hallway and onto the street below.

In 1968, few could help victims of childhood trauma because:

1. There was not yet a paradigm for understanding the problem;

2. Acknowledgement of responsibility for creation of the problem was not required from parents; and

3. No social validation of the serious, life-threatening consequences of family violence was in evidence, since it was not yet even a permissible topic of public conversation.

———·◦•———

The majority of abused children, adult survivors, and perpetrators still do not receive adequate help. Therapists are being trained, but our legal, social service, and educational systems lag far behind in that our belief system about "domestic" violence still hasn't changed. When our thinking about the problem really changes, funding priorities will change as well, and reform and services will be better supported.

If there is inadequate treatment after the fact, there is even less effort toward prevention of family violence. Colleges and training systems do not require that the effects of childhood trauma be taught to those studying to treat its survivors. As a consequence, those in the helping professions most needing the knowledge are untrained, often in denial, and therefore incapable of being the advocates their clients require.

Political and social institutions that are meant to help and protect the victimized are flawed and outmoded, and frequently serve only to reinforce the abusive behavior of the family of origin. The sheer numbers of dysfunctional people requiring services are leading to a breakdown in all our major institutions, including medical facilities, the courts, prisons, social services, and schools. "Burn-out" is incapacitating the most dedicated workers. People realize these systems are not designed properly, but no one seems able to resolve their dysfunction because it so perfectly mirrors the abuse of power by dysfunctional parents in relating to their children, a fact which everyone has tacitly agreed to keep secret. If anyone has the audacity to start talking about that parallel in an attempt to correctly name the problem and begin to attack it at its core, chances are that they will find themselves in hot water or even out of a job.

In 1992, at a luncheon in Washington, D.C., honoring police officers in child protective services, I met an attractive woman in her late thirties who introduced herself as a physician in pediatrics. She related that for several years she had been one of only two medical doctors in her county performing examinations on children reported to have been physically or sexually abused. She worked for the county Health Services Department, which served a population of several million. Not only did she perform the physical examinations, she also took the family medical histories and talked with the children about the events that lead to their coming to her office. Her reports later would be used as evidence if allegations of abuse were brought to court. It was with obvious distress that she disclosed that she was no longer at that job.

When I asked why, she replied that for several years her immediate supervisor, also a woman, had been trying to block the effectiveness of her work, making the workplace miserable in the hopes that the young physician would quit. When one tactic did not succeed, another was initiated. One day the physician was told that her position was to be entirely eliminated in a "budget cut." Soon the Health Services Department for that county, which served millions of people, did not have even one physician to examine children suspected of being abused. There would be no impartial observation of the facts, no medical evidence for the courts.

Colleagues from her department congratulated her on her *retirement*. When she told them her job had been eliminated, supposedly as a budget-cutting measure, her friends were very surprised. In a lowered voice, the doctor added, "I think my supervisor was abused as a child herself, and she wanted the issue dropped so that she did not have to face it every day at work." This is a perfect example of "system sabotage" by which the messenger and the message are disposed of at the same time.

When I am asked if I think we, as a society, have made much progress combatting violence and abuse over the past fifteen years, I have to answer,

NO. Transformation must occur both in the behavior of individuals and in social systems organization in order for us as a nation to begin reversing the trend of increasing violence from which we all suffer.

None of our social systems were originally designed to handle the consequences of such massive violence, not to mention the collapse of the traditional American family. None of these systems was designed to handle the numbers of people needing food, shelter, and long-term care, or the incarceration of the largest per capita prison population in the world.

Our social care systems were designed to deal with extreme hardship in limited time frames. They were intended as emergency systems, not as permanent care institutions. They were never designed to replace the family or the community, though that is increasingly the role they are forced to play. As the situations created by violence have worsened, they either have not had the time or have not recognized the necessity to restructure for the long haul.

We are faced with the double-edged problem of the violence of commission, actual violent behavior toward others, and the violence of omission, which takes the form of denial, neglect, and indifference. Violating behaviors result from violence itself, from fear of facing the cause of violence, and from self-involved indifference to the plight of anyone else.

Violence is indirectly or directly promoted in political language and by gun lobbies, hate groups, irresponsible media, intolerant religious organizations, various local and national government policies, and the individual behavior of millions of people, young and old, incapable or unwilling to face reality.

When large systems begin to crumble, we can view it as either a great danger or a new opportunity.

If we ignore the breakdown, we face the kind of destruction we saw in the Los Angeles rebellion. Many of our large cities are just an arm's length away from such an outburst of anger, and the rest of the country's population outside the cities is fully armed and intending to protect themselves.

———

In 1981, at the age of forty-two, my life took an unexpected "time out". Without warning, early one August morning, I had a massive stroke from which the medical experts did not expect recovery.

It was five years into my second marriage which, though very different from the first, was still not going well. I seemed not to have the capacity to say no and make it stick. I had no boundaries. Financially, I had done well after years of struggle, and for that I was grateful. I very much enjoyed the gift of a stepson and seeing him grow strong and healthy. My happiest moments were those around our family life, moments I'd never experienced before. The outside world, however, was filled with almost unbearable stress.

Mommie Dearest was a huge bestseller, topping the charts for nearly a year in hardcover, months more in paperback. My second book was finished and ready to go to press after a series of rewrites. The film version of my first book was complete.

I had enjoyed none of it, except the writing. Success was overshadowed by having to cope with the furor surrounding it. Going from a very private existence to this extremely public and controversial one was almost too much. Interviewers grilled me, TV comics made fun of me. Violence at home became an issue on the national agenda. By and large, the public understood, because so many millions of them had had similar experiences. As they began to come forward and to find the courage to speak out, the focus finally moved off me and onto the magnitude of the problem.

I had been wondering how to relieve the terrible amount of stress in my life, but having a massive stroke was not one of the options under consideration. One day I was fine, fully functional, running a business, a career, a home, and a ranch, and the next day I was paralyzed on my right side and unable to walk, speak, read, write, or think. I was in a near-vegetative state from the brain damage suffered.

When I first saw myself in the mirror a week after leaving home in an ambulance, after undergoing a complicated and never completed operation, I was in total shock. As I later wrote, "I looked like the lone surviving soldier of fierce combat on a battlefield I barely remembered. But, judging by the extent of my wounds, it had been a hell of a war."[1]

My entire life so far had been a hell of a war!

During the next four years of recovery, I spent most of my time alone. Once I could walk, I spent many months in the company of my dogs, learning about the wilderness around the ranch I shared with my business partner.

A new appreciation for processes, as opposed to results, began to grow out of my own painfully slow but persistent recovery. Physical abilities—walking, dressing, speaking—were the first to return. Mental or cognitive abilities came more slowly. Gaining coordinated use of both my hands came very slowly indeed. Thinking, comprehension of written material, problem solving, and creativity were the last skills restored to me, and only after five or six years.

I had recurring aphasia (inability to think or speak clearly), so that all tasks needed to be reduced to their smallest component parts if I wanted to accomplish them. My undamaged brain cells were literally being reprogrammed with new information and new skills. Doctors and therapists told me that it was vitally important to feed my brain only the best and most correct information, so that "garbage" would not interfere with this learning process. There could be no sloppiness, no short-cuts. The process demanded seemingly endless amounts of patience. Patience seemed to be one of the major lessons of my whole life and now I would finally have to learn it or face the prospect of not recovering.

This illness was forcing me to relearn every skill originally acquired in childhood: eating, speaking, using silverware, brushing teeth, tying shoes, doing buttons, dressing, bathing, reading, writing, using a telephone, working with numbers, etc.

In this process, all the other experiences of my childhood associated with learning, including old feelings long hidden away and forgotten, resurfaced with sudden clarity. Some of the feelings were extremely painful, such as the humiliation I felt when I couldn't get a task right the first time I tried it. I was also beset by feelings of awkwardness, unlovability, loneliness, and being damaged in ways I didn't comprehend, and being scared, very, very scared.

These emotions challenged me to re-examine childhood experiences as well as how my past and present would determine who I could be in the world that awaited me when I chose to return to it. It was a difficult, painful, illuminating process.

Since I did not speak well at first, the learning process took place experientially, on a physical level and through communication with myself and with the natural world in which I spent the majority of my time. Plants and animals did not seem to mind if my words weren't right.

I walked the fields and woodlands, sat by the creeks, prayed to the stars and the land, cried my tears, and tried to listen to my intuition while I paid close attention to my feelings and thoughts.

This illness and my recovery from it connected me with my own body in ways that I'd not experienced before. As a child, I had learned to think of my own body as foreign and distant in order to endure the pain and humiliation inflicted upon it. As I grew up, my body became a possession to decorate and keep thin, but not a source of wellness, joy, or intimacy.

Now I experienced each muscle, each finger, every new movement of coordination with awe. I learned to respect my own body. I learned to respect myself. I felt I knew myself for the very first time in my entire life. What a revelation it was to me to see how cut off from myself I had been all those years. No wonder I had been sick so much. No wonder I had permitted myself to smoke even after having pneumonia. No wonder I starved myself and had sex with people I didn't like. No wonder I hadn't seemed to know what colors or what styles of clothing looked best on me. As I learned how my body worked and gained respect for it, there was no problem in knowing what colors I liked, what clothes I wanted to wear, what food I preferred to feed myself.

Once the physical aspects of my new being began to heal, I began to work on the cognitive and psychological levels.

No longer numb to myself, very often the enormity of what had happened to me was overwhelming. For months I did not want to leave home or be in contact with new people. I had to find new names by which to define the people and events of my childhood and adolescence. I could no longer refer to the woman who adopted me as Mother because she was not. I found the real name for the violations to my mind and body and called them what they actually were: rape, terrorism, torture, attempted murder, abandonment—the list was long.

I realized how much I had missed in childhood. I had missed the chance to be a child. I had missed the chance to be loved as a child. I had missed the opportunity to learn as a child, so that I would be prepared for the adult world when I got there. And I had missed much of my early adulthood because my time and energy were consumed with trying to cope with the effects of the past.

In June of 1985, on my forty-sixth birthday, I came to another stunning revelation: even after so many years and so much intensive work on myself, I still did not know how to be a person!

My re-entry into the world held yet another rude awakening for me: there was almost no money left from what I had previously earned, no career after five years of not being able to work, and no husband either. It was a mighty scramble to salvage even a place in which to live.

Yet, once again I survived. Surviving was what I knew best about life.

In coming back to life, I had already beaten nearly insurmountable odds, so I determined that neither the debts nor my not knowing how to be a person were adequate excuses for giving up. If it took me the rest of whatever time I had left, I was determined to unravel the treacherous knot that kept me and so many others in misery.

As that understanding surfaced in my learning process, I knew I had to share it. The first step towards that goal was accomplished with the publication of my third book, *Survivor*, in 1988. Also autobiographical, it covered the ten years after *Mommie Dearest* through my recovery from the stroke.

———

A sad surprise waited for me when finally I returned to the world to find work, earn a living, write, and create a new life for myself: violence was everywhere.

)rugs had taken precedence over inquiry into what was
tiable demand for drugs. Public funds were spent prima-
my o.. -   prisons and prosecuting criminals, with little left over for
the victims. No more than lip service was paid to the need for prevention
of violence.

Now, in the 1990s, we still do not hear much about the causes of violence.
Research has been published in all fields relating to the problem; we are
flooded with facts and data; yet facing the core of violence, the connection
between what happens in the home (abuse, trauma) and what then happens
on the street, in the boardrooms and bar rooms, in places of work, and then
again in families—that has not yet been accomplished.

Former Washington, D.C., police chief Isaac Fulwood remarked in a speech
in the city with the highest per capita murder rate in the country:[2] "We know
how to get them [guns and drugs] off the streets, but there's no will to do it."[3]

Why do we not have the will to tackle and solve this problem?

—Because too many of us have known violence firsthand. We have been
either its victims or its perpetrators. Once we as abused children numb
ourselves to the experience at home, we set in motion the ability to shut out
other disturbing information as well. And those who benefit from the use of
violence will not want to voluntarily give up the sense of power over others
it gives them, and so they will fight to protect their "rights" to it.

If, in the course of growing up, you were terrorized, and no one let you
know that the trauma you were suffering was wrong and should not be
happening, you as an adult may still be unable to recognize and grieve the
losses of your past and to release your justifiable anger for what was done
to you. In this case, the process of healing cannot really begin and, instead,
the numbing continues, for the pain it is masking is usually too terrifying to
unravel alone.

If no one ever took your side, defended you, cared for you, chances are that
you will not feel able to defend or protect yourself in adulthood. You may
also feel unable to protect anyone else, including your own children.

It is a dreadfully circular dilemma. And meanwhile, the violence continues.

The root problem of violence is described by the epithet, "As you sow, so
shall you reap." If children are treated with violence and disrespect, that's
what they learn and reenact, either at home with their own children, or in the
larger arena of community and society.

If home is not a safe place, then nowhere else on earth can be safe.

The Survivor's Wheel

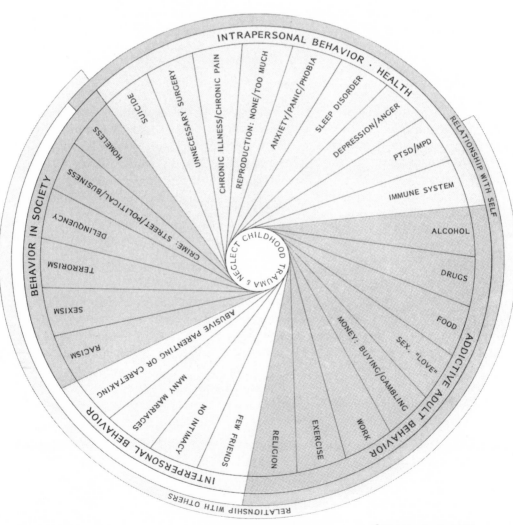

© Christina Crawford 1991

CHAPTER 2

The Survivor's Wheel

Across from the Viet Nam Memorial Wall on Constitution Avenue in Washington, D.C., is the National Academy of Science where, in a beautifully landscaped flower garden, the Einstein Memorial is located. Behind a grove of holly and elm trees, one comes upon an informally seated bronze figure of Einstein gazing down at a celestial map of the universe and holding a paper on which are inscribed his famous mathematical equations. There are several quotations from his writing. "As long as I have any choice in the matter, I shall live only in a country where civil liberty, tolerance, and equality of all citizens before the law prevail," reads one. Another: "The right to search for truth implies also a duty: one must not conceal any part of what one has recognized to be true."

The Survivor's Wheel, pictured on the preceeding page, evolved out of my search for the truth and understanding of my own history and that of other survivors of family violence. I pieced it together bit by bit from years of observation, research, and life experience. With each piece came increased understanding of the relationship between the trauma of violence in childhood and dysfunctional behaviors in adulthood.

The Survivor's Wheel is a graphic representation of a wide range of dysfunctional behaviors, of various forms of violence against self, others, and society at large and how they relate to childhood abuse and neglect and to each other. It visually links the causes and effects of these behaviors so that one can gain insight as to why events in one's life took shape as they did. The individual moves from one behavior to another over time, shedding and adding. This interplay of survivor behaviors, as illustrated by the Wheel, constitutes a clearly recognizable condition, which I call Complex Survivor Syndrome (CSS).

The Wheel is predictive in the sense that certain survivor behaviors will inevitably result if the core issues of childhood trauma and abuse are not dealt with. With a turn of the Wheel, chances are a survivor will identify with at least one spoke or behavior. When there is one, then look for at least one more, perhaps in an entirely different section. Notice how the two or more behaviors meet at the Hub, represent childhood trauma and neglect. Thus the Wheel effectively describes violence as an organizing principle between generations.

The Survivor's Wheel also outlines the structure of the main body of this book. Beginning with addictions and moving around the Wheel through intrapersonal and health issues, we will explore each survivor behavior as it evolves from the core childhood experience of family violence and into other personal behavior patterns. The cycle of violence can begin with any of the behaviors, however, so one can enter the Survivor's Wheel equally effectively at any spoke.

The Wheel has various component parts:

Categories

There are four major categories into which these coping or victimizing behaviors are grouped. They are:

- Intrapersonal behaviors;
- Addictive behaviors;
- Interpersonal behaviors; and
- Behaviors in society.

These four categories fall into two larger groupings: behaviors reflecting relationship with self and behaviors reflecting relationship with others. Naturally, there is overlap and interaction between them.

The Hub

The hub of the wheel represents the original childhood experience of trauma and neglect in a violent family. This experience precedes the development of all survivor behaviors emanating out from it.

The hub is the source of all subsequent survivor behaviors. It is the experience that we as survivors carry with us of a family of origin that was neglectful of our needs, absent as protector or caretaker, disrespectful of our personal boundaries, and abusive to our bodies, minds, and/or spirits.

ιe wheel represent coping behaviors that were developed
with victimization, anger, and feelings of emptiness.
Unapp̳̳   ney may seem to others, these behaviors, at least at one time,
were vital to survivors' efforts to stay alive and to cope with the insanity
around them, which they could not change and against which they could not
defend themselves.

Efforts to give up these behaviors without new ones to substitute for them
usually meet with failure.

If the direction of movement through spokes of the Wheel is reversed,
these same behaviors are seen to spiral in to act upon the core, the child's
developmental process, where they become perpetrating or abusive. Thus the
spokes of the Wheel, depending on directionality, represent either the coping
behaviors developed by the child for survival or the victimizing behaviors of
adults that negatively impact the child's development: they can be either
cause or effect.

Thus the Wheel also shows generational cycles in which one generation's
coping behaviors become the next generation's victimization. (This same
dynamic holds true in politics, business, and social systems.)

The spokes are fluid and interactive. They are dynamic, rather than static
or fixed. People may activate different behaviors at different times. They may
"fix" or solve one, only to find themselves struggling with another, never
realizing the relationship between these symptoms and other life problems.

Without addressing the core issue of childhood abuse, life can be only
symptoms management, a frustrating and disheartening process in which the
survivor moves from one symptom or behavior to another, from addiction
management to pain management to abusive relationships, shedding and
adding, in perpetual chaos, without ever understanding why life is such a mess.

Adult life for the survivor may "run on automatic." Someone inadvertently or intentionally pushes the button of an old childhood fear, threatens
abandonment or pain, and the survivor reacts the same way he or she did as
a child facing similar consequences. Unfortunately, until the original trauma
is unearthed and faced, the survivor will remain programmed for abuse. Abuse
over time is a form of death. Survivors often exist more dead than alive.

Most survivors will not receive therapeutic assistance, either because they
will not ask for it, or because, when they do ask, they will not be understood.

Before becoming survivors, we were victims. We became victims by suffering events that were beyond personal control and from which it was

impossible to flee without incurring further harm. To be a victim is to be a target for the behavior of others with greater power who are willing to use that power against us.

A victim is the recipient of the behavior of others and reacts to it.

A survivor initiates behavior in order to make personal progress and solve problems.

We who were systemically terrorized in childhood developed self-protective skills and conduct that include:

• Observation of others in order to foretell danger;

• Avoidance of pain by any means;

• When avoidance fails, pleasing (appeasing) the abuser to minimize pain;

• Total disregard of our own *feelings;*

• Total disregard of our own *needs;*

• Total disregard of our own *bodies.*

As children we could do nothing more. We didn't know how.

As children we could do nothing less. We wanted to live. We were programmed as children to tolerate, if not actually accept, abusive behavior. Our selves needed defending, but we were too little to do it. When we could neither protect ourselves nor run away, other forms of escape from pain were devised. These make the spokes of the Survivor's Wheel.

Until very recently, adult behaviors such as alcoholism, chronic pain, eating or sleep disorders, crime, and suicide were seen exclusively as adult problems unrelated to a person's childhood experience and isolated one from the other and from the totality of the person.

In our current health care system, professionals specialize in treating different symptoms. Most professionals do not exchange information outside their own field of specialization. Our educational system encourages reductionist thinking rather than seeing oneself and others as multi-dimensional and changing over time.

Because the concept that childhood experiences have long-term consequences has met with so much resistance, few professionals called upon to help child victims or adult survivors feel the necessity to resolve their own family of origin problems. Thus they may inadvertently contribute through their own survivor behaviors to the exploitation, re-victimization, fraud, humiliation, or disrespect of their clients.

Often survivors develop only those skills required for survival. They often lack other ordinary relationship skills, and so they trust professionals when they should question them, they believe without sufficient reason and then feel betrayed, they become enraged when they really need to cry, and they withdraw when they most need help. Their reactions are inappropriate: too much, too little, too soon, or too late.

Stages of Healing

The process of freeing oneself from entanglement with the past takes place gradually and needs time. It is necessary to go through all the steps, feelings, and learning tasks if one is to emerge from past programming and to move beyond life on the Survivor's Wheel. Skipping stages in an attempt to hurry the process may actually slow it down. Short cuts do not work because they do not allow for integration of new skills and detoxification from poisonous early experiences. Short cuts build shaky foundations, leaving the person less able to let go and go on.

Many have written about the various stages of change, but almost all agree on the following basic pattern:

- Shock/trauma
- Anger/fear
- Denial/withdrawal
- Anger/rage
- Grief/sadness
- Problem solving
- Acceptance/letting go of the past

Because each stage of change involves strong emotions, it is a demanding process, whether it is oneself or someone close who is going through it. For almost everyone, it feels like a kind of death. In a way, that is an accurate description, for one must let the old life drop away before a new life can come into being.

The Three "R's"

The Three R's describe an approach that I have created by which the survivor can begin to create a new foundation for living. It involves three aspects: *renaming*, or finding new words to express what actually took place in early life and filling in the memory gaps; *reframing*, or readjusting the context in which one understands what happened so that it becomes believable; and *reclaiming* one's own life.

- *Renaming*: What literally and accurately happer
  simplest words? The stark facts are stated with(
  guilty. What, where, when, by whom, and for h
  survivor may need to ask a lot of questions and
  information about his or her life, health, past, an ﹍ ﹍ people
  who have shared it.

- *Reframing*: The survivor comes to believe the facts unearthed
  and does not dismiss them as figments of his or her imagination. The survivor learns to trust his or her intuition and believe
  him/herself. Believe that it hurt. Believe that there have been
  long-term consequences to his/her life because of what happened. See those consequences as deserving neither blame nor
  shame.

- *Reclaiming*: The survivor comes to understand that years of his/
  her life have been consumed in trying to survive childhood
  trauma and that that time has been lost for other purposes. The
  survivor reclaims those years in some special and meaningful
  ways after allowing him/herself to feel the grief that loss always
  carries with it. The survivor comes to believe they can now fill
  in the blank spaces and empty places, replace turbulent relationships with healthy ones, and create a new life.

Renaming is the most difficult and crucial of these three stages. When
anyone controls the language of a society, they can control its behavior. All
despotic governments know this, which is why, in the process of a take-over,
they seize control of the communications systems first. In giving true names
to what happened, the survivor may find him/herself fighting the myths and
masquerades of entrenched social conventions.

To begin to rename abusers' actions and behaviors, the feelings observed
in and evoked by them, and the nature of family interactions is a major first
step toward healing. The truth can set us free.

The Scope of the Damage

Long-term damage results from overt acts of violence such as beating,
rape, terrorizing, and prolonged deprivation and neglect of children, spouses,
and prison inmates. Damage also results from the more subtle forms of
violence found in business practices, politics, military life, the law, schools,
churches, and on the street. Those subtle forms include humiliation, criticism,
seduction, dehumanization, and raging. Violence may see-saw between overt

nd covert behaviors; but in all forms of violence, the three demons of drugs, alcohol, and physical or mental illness are likely to be present.

Violence is rarely a single incident; it is a way of life. As such, it is always expected, always anticipated. It is this constant anticipation that accelerates the internalization of violence and oppression. As the child grows older, violence is incorporated as an integral part of self-image, self-esteem, self-concept, and world view.

As long as the victim/survivor remains isolated and without belief in the possibility of choosing a different way of life, he or she in some way will remain trapped in the abuses of the family and society, in denial of the core problem, and vulnerable to internalized violence and the coping behaviors of the Survivor's Wheel.

The Survivor's Wheel has no place, however, in an atmosphere of truth, compassion, personal responsibility, and patience with the process of change. When we neither participate in violence nor condone it in others, violence will release its present stranglehold on our society.

Addictive Behavior

CHAPTER 3

Addictive Behavior

That America is a highly addictive society is clearly illustrated by the Survivor's Wheel. Addiction is one of the most recognizable behaviors for coping with or perpetrating violence.

Preliminary research indicates a close correlation between childhood abuse and later addictions and between the severity of the trauma and the number of addictive behaviors.[1] It seems to have come as a surprise to researchers that family violence and addiction are related, but not to those of us who have lived with that truth.

All addictive behaviors are initially rewarding. Addiction is about avoiding pain. No matter how destructive their consequences may be later on, addictions initially are experienced as self-soothing, and the absence of them is felt as a great loss.

Addictions are the deeply entrenched coping behaviors that have permitted the survivor to continue to live. When carried to their limit, they all lead to disaster, even death; yet the survivor sees them as enabling life. Addictions always lead to a life-or-death struggle.

Addictive behaviors seem nearly to erase all lines of demarcation between what one does to oneself and what that does to one's family, friends, and associates.

In specific cultural settings, addictions become so prevalent as to be considered "normal." It is then nearly impossible to intervene, because no one is aware of any problem. The tendency, then, is to focus on something external, anything other than the addiction as the cause for whatever failure, ill health, or turmoil is experienced.

Some addicts will practice addiction management, going from one addictive behavior to the next, never letting any one get totally out of control. Pretty soon, they are back to the original addiction in a spiraling effect of ever-increasing addictive activity that eventually spirals out of control. The addict usually has no comprehension of what lies at the root of this chaotic lifestyle that careens from drinking, to spending, to dieting, to exercise, to working too hard, to sex. While some lives may look like fast-track successes and others may look like chaotic messes, the key is sustainability: lives built around most addictions are not sustainable. Workaholism may be the only exception. Most other addictions have such seriously negative consequences that they destroy the addict's body within five to ten years, sometimes (as with crack cocaine) much sooner.

Pursuing one addiction after another only to discover that the "empty place" within still is not filled leads to a sense of frantic, usually silent despair. The external violence from which one sought to escape becomes internalized as violence against oneself.

Two-thirds of our economy is fueled by the consumer rather than by manufacturing or other business sectors. Advertising and television create the impression that buying and spending are values in themselves. They constantly reinforce the need for instant gratification from products outside oneself, which is the very foundation of addictive behavior.

Over and above the personal dedication and patience required to plan another way of life, the addict must find ways to counteract society's mixed messages, such as public service spots saying, "Don't drink and drive," followed only minutes later by a TV commercial showing sexy guys at a party drinking Brand X beer, getting the girl, and driving away in a hot, sporty car. Then the next ad recommends taking a pill for instant relief from the symptom, never mind its cause. This pattern is repeated hundreds of times every day.

Should the addict choose recovery, he or she then will face the task of creating, without much support from others, an alternative way of being in the world. He or she may have to move to a new location and find new friends who are themselves not active addicts. Family gatherings may become impossible and may have to be avoided for a time if other family members deny the problems or enable them to continue unchecked. People may not want to hear about your progress because they are jealous or stuck themselves. There may be times of extreme loneliness after the dysfunctional lifestyle has been relinquished, but before the new, healthier one has taken shape. Support groups are helpful. Like-minded friends are inspirational. Compassion for self is essential.

Alcoholism

An estimated ten percent of American adults have a drinking problem and forty-three percent are exposed to alcoholism through family or marriage. Twenty-seven million American adults grew up with an alcoholic parent.[2]

When I was growing up, alcoholism was not recognized as a disease. Almost everyone in my world drank alcohol regularly. A number of my school friends and classmates also had parents who drank heavily and with whom they had a great deal of difficulty. We talked amongst ourselves in whispered voices about what our parents did to us and themselves when they were drinking. We wondered what, if anything, we could do to lessen the pain and fear of being with them. We rarely spoke about the problem with teachers or school principals, although many of them sensed there was something wrong at home.

Thirty years would pass before what we experienced was named and addressed directly by recovery programs for adult children of alcoholics. Today there are nearly 1,000 self-help Adult Children of Alcoholics (ACA) meetings across America every week.

Back in the 1950s, we had to fend for ourselves. We felt ashamed of our parents and their inappropriate public behavior and made excuses to cover for them. We felt scared and humiliated by their private behavior and violent outbursts, and bewildered by their lack of feeling and memory for what they had done when drunk. I tried many times to alert adults at boarding school to my mother's mercurial shifts. I explained how she acted when she'd been drinking and I advised them, sometimes pleaded with them, not to call her in the evening when her anger and irrationality would most likely be at their worst.

Unfortunately, they did not take my advice until it was too late to avert the chaos. For me, that chaos took form in bizarre punishments such as taking away all my clothes but two dresses to wear for five months, or requiring that I be given extra work or that I remain at boarding school over holidays and summer when everyone else went home. In effect, she demanded that the school authorities keep me in a jail-like atmosphere, which they did, even though no one believed I'd done anything wrong. I never understood my teachers' refusal to listen to me and I deeply resented their willful ignorance of my problem. I was left totally alone to cope with my mother's violence. Today the behavior of the school authorities would be called denial.

Denial is society's silent permission for addiction and violence to continue unchecked. People in denial act as though nothing is wrong. Denial in community endangers others because it enables groups of people to behave violently without social policies and programs in place to stop them. Denial ensures a "business as usual" attitude even as everything falls apart before one's very eyes.

When I was a teenager, my adoptive mother frequently drove with a plastic water glass filled with ice and 100-proof vodka wedged between her knees. Sometimes she asked me to pour her a refill or to hold the glass for her until she was ready to drink it. She drove very fast. It scared me, but I could not refuse to go with her, nor could I refuse to fix the drink unless I wanted both physical and emotional punishment for "disobeying." I never saw nor heard any adult in her world challenge her or say that drinking and driving was dangerous behavior.

Never in my teens, twenties, or thirties did I believe the insidious nature of alcohol had seriously affected me. Only later did I learn that my entire relationship to my own life had been shaped by my relationship with an alcoholic. Long after there was no further physical contact between my mother and myself, I continued to operate with the destructive values and behaviors learned from an alcoholic in the early years of my childhood.

My first drinks were given to me by my mother. I was ordered to make mixed drinks of hard liquor for adult guests visiting our house from the time I was eight or nine years old. Sometimes I made them too strong on purpose just to see what would happen. They just teased me a little and got drunk quicker.

I was given drinks in restaurants in the company of family from the age of fourteen. I was drinking at luncheons by the age of sixteen. My adoptive mother had me drink with her when she was lonely. I learned to use alcohol as "company," to ward off anxiety and loneliness, to fill up the empty place.

Because I didn't think my behavior was as out of control as my mother's, I had no idea that alcohol might be a problem in my life. Sometimes it was, sometimes it was not, sometimes I drank, sometimes I did not drink, depending on what was going on in my life. For a while I attended Alcoholics Anonymous meetings. After two years, I stopped. Alcohol is still an unsettled issue in my life.

Having grown up in an alcoholic family, a survivor may suffer greatly as an adult—whether he or she drinks or not—and not realize that the root cause of the unhappiness lies in childhood experience of alcoholism as the organizing principle for all family interactions. The survivor may still be in denial about the extent of his/her parents' destructive behavior. Since he/she has no understanding as to what has gone wrong or how to reshape his/her life, at some point this person may begin to believe that others have caused his/her unhappiness. In time, this belief turns into bitterness and isolation.

Some active alcoholics have to lose everything before deciding either to die or live sober. At that point, they are ready for family intervention, a care unit, or Alcoholics Anonymous.

I have learned that most people will not relinquish an addictive behavior until it is clear it will have such serious, even life-threatening, consequences that to change, frightening as that may be, is preferable. When the fear of the unknown is less than the fear of the present, change can take seed.

Most people today have access to information about the reasonable and responsible use of alcohol, but because it is legal and relatively inexpensive, it is still the number one addiction of choice.

When a woman consumes alcohol during pregnancy, fetal alcohol syndrome (FAS) frequently results. FAS is now recognized as the cause of birth defects, brain damage, learning disabilities, and a number of other impairments to the fetus and infant.[3] Upwards of 10,000 babies are diagnosed each year with FAS. The number of infants affected actually may be much higher, because few hospitals test for FAS, even in very low birthweight babies.

Fetal alcohol syndrome causes brain cells in the afflicted fetus to be organized differently from those of a normal fetus. The damage is irreversible, as far as we know. The FAS child has difficulty controlling emotions, learning, concentrating, and bonding. We are now learning, primarily from families who have adopted these children, that the onset of their delinquent behavior, as differentiated from psychological and learning problems, is in adolescence. It is then that these children start hurting others, setting fires, and getting into trouble at school.

A recent study of Fetal Alcohol Syndrome by a team of doctors at the University of Washington Medical School concluded that FAS should be "considered a lifelong disorder," and not just the physical and mental abnormality of an infant born to a woman who consumed alcohol while pregnant.

"Gestational exposure to alcohol can cause a wide spectrum of disabilities that have lifelong physical, mental, and behavior implication." The doctors' findings in the April 1991 *Journal of American Medical Association* included these characteristics of the FAS child:

- an average IQ of 68, when the norm is 100;
- learning ability between second and fourth grade levels when the child is beyond those grades in age;

- deficiency in math skills;
- maladaptive behaviors, such as short attention span, poor judgment, and problems with social interaction.

Most study participants were between the ages of twelve and forty and had not been diagnosed as having FAS when they were infants.

The researchers urged the educational system and local communities to recognize the need to provide these people with special schooling, job training, and housing to "prevent victimization, dysfunctional lives, increased psychopathology, chronic mental illness, and homelessness."[4]

The cost of treatment of such cases is over $321 million per year.[5]

This is a tragic example of the interaction between one generation's coping behavior and the next generation's victimization. It is also a perfect demonstration of the interconnectedness between different spokes of the Survivor's Wheel.

The mother's addictive use of alcohol impacts the fetus *in utero* so that the child develops maladaptively physically, mentally, and socially. If the child has not been diagnosed as having FAS, the child's dysfunctional behavior in school will likely be seen as solely his/her own fault.

Growing up, the child will be condemned by his/her failures. The child's aberrant behavior will not be understood as stemming from the mother's behavior before his/her birth. The boy or girl will not understand why he/she cannot make positive progress in life. It is a tragedy, but a preventable one.

The last person in the generational cycle to come to the attention of authority is always the one faulted; but it is the behavior of parents, caretakers, health care workers, community members, and government employees that creates the conditions under which the child is provided a *less* than minimal chance of developing healthily. The child can do nothing about pre-existing conditions; he or she is not responsible for creating them and may not be able to overcome them.

Much can be done to prevent the incidence of FAS by educating people before they become parents, by detoxifying and treating addicts, and by providing minimal health care to pregnant mothers. The up-front costs of prevention are always well spent, particularly when compared to the costs of crime, prisons, and wasted lives. But until politicians and the public understand the long-term effects of addictive behavior on the next generation, prevention will continue to take a back seat to prison building.

For both the young and old, alcohol is a serious problem.

Teenage drinking has always been hazardous, particularly when combined with driving. Today large numbers of fatalities are resulting from marathon weekend parties at which young people consume large amounts of alcohol very quickly and then die from respiratory and heart failure.

Teenagers are calling themselves "weekend alcoholics" with some glee. They talk quite openly about "pressure" in their lives and how "living for the moment" is all there is to life.

An estimated ten percent of adults over sixty years old have problems with alcohol.[6] Some of those have been drinking for years, but as the alcoholic ages, there are increasing health problems, broken bones, and family disputes. Of particular concern in older people is the combination of alcohol with other prescription medications they may be taking, such as those for blood pressure or sleeping.

Other seniors who rarely or never drank previously may begin after the death of a loved one or because of loneliness and boredom in retirement. In just a few years these people may find themselves in sad shape, because, with age, the body becomes less able to detoxify rapidly and consequently less tolerant of alcohol. These recent converts to alcohol have an excellent chance for complete recovery from addiction if they receive prompt treatment and attend follow-up meetings.

Betty Ford, wife of former President Gerald Ford, by publishing her book and opening her clinic in Palm Springs, California, has inspired and helped thousands to successfully change their lives. In all parts of the country there are free self-help groups and AA meetings. Care units and detoxification programs, usually reimbursed by insurance, can be found in most areas. Books are plentiful. Help is readily available if one wants it.

Drug Addiction

Drugs and violence in the United States today are inseparable in the minds of public and government alike. When violence is a way of life, the demand for drugs is apparently insatiable. Where drugs are used and sold, violence assures payment and territorial supremacy.

But it was not always so. Originally, most mood-altering substances were used ceremonially, in healing and religious rituals.

Rarely were drugs used outside a healing or spiritual context, just for recreational pleasure.

Every culture has had its "home brew," its psychedelic plants and related rituals. And every generation has had individuals at various levels in society who have overindulged. Some users were of great genius (e.g., Mozart) while others have died anonymously under a bridge.

The United States has a long history of using both "home-brewed" and manufactured drugs. In the 1800s and again at the turn of the century, opium dens flourished in New York and San Francisco. In the South, field workers were paid part of their weekly salaries in small bags of cocaine, or "coke," which then became the nickname for a local beverage.

In the 1960s, when I first lived in New York City as an eighteen year-old teenager on my own, the primary street drugs were marijuana and heroin. Uppers and downers could be had in pill form and were often passed from friend to friend, much as marijuana was handled at that time. Marijuana was in such common use that people grew it in their backyards among their tomato plants or in flower pots under grow lights. Money was only rarely involved in obtaining a supply, and consequently there was little incentive for gang involvement or violence.

No one, in fact, paid much attention to the use of "grass," although it was illegal. Marijuana was rarely involved in violence among either users or sellers.

In contrast, heroin was big business, and violence was its trademark. Police raided sellers, arrested users, and the churches in both black and Spanish East Harlem posted weekly death counts of victims outside on their signs above the service times and pastor's name.

I knew musicians and some street people who shot heroin. Nothing was more important to them than their habit. They stole from and lied to friends, needing more and more of the drug, just to stay "straight," and usually ended up either in prison on Riker's Island or dead. Neither junkies nor heroin were glamorous.

By 1962, when I went back to California to work, the new drug of choice was LSD. (Today its use is once again on the rise among young people who can buy a "trip" for five dollars.) A number of my friends dropped acid and were never the same again. It had such strange effects on them that I resolved not to try it.

Cocaine, a stimulant, soon followed heroin as the drug of choice. It became the chic drug, the upper class drug, the "in" drug. The use of cocaine was so open in Los Angeles during the 1970s that people snorted it at the table in restaurants. There was a sort of cocaine elite in the entertainment industry: you either used it and provided it as a sweetener for business deals or you found yourself "out." In fact, the very widespread use of drugs was one of the reasons many independent producers and directors left Los Angeles to work on locations elsewhere. It became very difficult to find crew members who were not on drugs, and those that were could not be fired, even when unreliable, if they were in the unions. Instead of fighting the system, many who were able to leave and work elsewhere did so.

Statistics may vary slightly, but it seems clear that the highly publicized War on Drugs has failed—not because millions of dollars in drugs have not been seized, and not because hundreds of dealers have not been put in prison, but because nothing has been done to address the demand for drugs in America.

Cocaine is used by an estimated 1.9 million to 2.2 million people per year. This represents an increase in use by those thirty-five and older, and a slight decrease in use by children twelve to seventeen years old.[7]

The increase in use is thought to be occurring in hard core drug users for whom treatment has either not been sought or not been effective, as well as in those who had stopped using and then "picked up" again. While the indicators on cocaine use show some positive signs, the news about heroin is all bad.

In 1991, fears surfaced of an epidemic of heroin use similar to the one in the sixties. Thirty years ago, heroin came primarily from Turkey through the French connection. Today the drugs come in much purer form from Southeast Asia. An estimated 750,000 Americans are now using heroin, and half of those users are in New York City. Southeast Asians, Chinese, and Columbian drug lords are all jockeying for control of this lucrative market. A kilogram of cocaine sells for about $20,000 in New York, while a kilogram of heroin (averaging about 40% to 50% purity on the street) sells for about $250,000.

Dealing street drugs is now the big money culture. It is the way out of poverty that used to be sought through careers in sports, music, education, or entertainment. With big money culture comes violence. The life span of dealers and users on the streets is probably about five years. After that, they are either hopeless and brain-fried, in prison, or dead.

PCP, crack cocaine, and "ice" are now cheaply manufactured for street use and priced to sell at under five dollars a hit. Each new synthetic drug is more damaging to the brain and body, more instantly addictive, and easier to obtain. All are sold and used in an atmosphere of violence.

In January 1991, the PBS program *MacNeill/Lehrer* reported on teenage crime, specifically murder, interviewing a New York City youth worker in the probation department, Angel Rodriguez. Mr. Rodriguez said that the kids he was seeing were being sexually abused and beaten by adults who were addicts and alcoholics. As a result of this brutal treatment by their parents, these children, according to Mr. Rodriguez, had "lost their sense of morality."[8] Without a sense of morality, they experienced no personal penalties for behavior, no sense of guilt, no difference between right and wrong except in terms of pay-offs. Many are surprised and even horrified by the commission of "senseless" crimes against strangers. The only way one can fit such crimes into a framework of understanding is to seek for answers beyond and before the "senselessness."

A federal study undertaken in Washington, D.C., and released in March 1991 showed that *one in three children in that city had been an eye-witness to a shooting or stabbing,* often of a family member or friend. How do children develop a "sense of morality" under those circumstances?

When I was Commissioner for Children's Services in Los Angeles during the late 1980s, I had the opportunity to speak with workers throughout the county system. In conversation with a worker in the probation department, I was told that their records indicated that all of the women on probation who had been convicted of drug-related crimes had previous histories of being sexually abused as children. From professional experience, they had discovered the connection between childhood violation and later drug use, even though no formal research studies yet existed on the subject.

The War on Drugs will never succeed as long as it concentrates on shutting down the *supply* of drugs. The battle against addiction cannot be won with guns and bloodshed, or in courts and prison cells. At the beginning of the 1980s, California had twelve prisons. A decade later, the state has twenty-three that cost 2.5 billion dollars to maintain—and more are being built.[9]

The number of drug-addicted babies born every week in cities across the country is staggering. If they survive withdrawal, they suffer pain, brain damage, and the life-long possibility of dysfunction. The cost to taxpayers is enormous, both at birth and later, because most of these babies do not return to mother after birth but are placed by the government in shelters and foster care.

These children come into the school systems at a rate of about 400,000 per year, often with learning problems, an impaired immune system, and behavioral difficulties such as short attention span, memory lapses, and inability to make friends or to meet minimum procedural requirements. Often these children evidence behavior that is associated with the sociopath.

New research indicates that when the biological father uses cocaine, his sperm carries the drug to the egg being fertilized, causing birth defects in the child. Dr. Randal Odem, Washington University School of Medicine in St. Louis, says, "Cocaine may be just the first of a long list of substances that are shown to bind to the sperm." While indicating the need for further study, Dr. Odem adds, "Sperm may be essentially a transport mechanism for drugs."[10] These findings carry further implications that men exposed to toxic chemicals and pesticides may be responsible for birth defects in their children, a suspicion also long held by Viet Nam veterans exposed to the defoliant Agent Orange.

Drug use and the AIDS disease are now well known to be interrelated. Unsterile, shared needles and unprotected sexual encounters spread AIDS. Bisexual men as well as prostitutes who are intravenous drug users have accelerated the transmission of AIDS into the heterosexual community and mainstream America. There are approximately one million female prostitutes visited by about twenty million men every year in the United States. Most prostitutes are drug users. A very large proportion of prostitutes were sexually abused as children.

In New York City, ten percent of live births are now AIDS babies. The cost to keep each child alive for one year is $100,000, all taxpayer money.[11] Health care workers are in danger of being infected by patients as well as infecting them. Patients are asked to indicate if they have tested HIV-positive, but doctors, dentists, and other health care workers as yet have not been similarly encouraged. Blood supplies are still being contaminated, and denial of the horror of AIDS still persists.

Some time ago I overheard a man say to a woman: "Let's get high and be somebody." It was the perfect description of addiction.

Eating Disorders

With the technological advancements of this century, we have become increasingly alienated from the source of our nourishment and less involved in producing our own food. We have lost touch with the need to respect the animals and plants that support our lives. We've forgotten that animals and fish have faces and eyes. We've forgotten that fruits and vegetables have rich, natural flavor and healing properties. We've forgotten about natural sweetness, natural fiber, natural crispness.

We've also forgotten about nursing babies and the human bond that is created during natural childbirth and breastfeeding. As a result, babies that have not been breastfed have lost both the nurturance from bonding with the mother and the immunization properties present in mother's milk during the first year of the baby's life. Instead, we've been propping babies in highchairs and leaving them alone to suck manufactured milk from plastic nipples.

Happily, such practices are now less often recommended, and mothers are strongly encouraged to breastfeed their infants for at least a year. Nourishment so directly received from the mother can be deeply satisfying, conveying love, intimacy, and a sense of connection to another human being.

Still, generations have grown to maturity not understanding that the process of nourishment is not merely chemical but involves feelings and physical contact as well as food. The mechanization of the nourishment process has left many people with the feeling of a terrible emptiness inside, an emptiness that sometimes feels insatiable. We try to fill the hole with junk food, fast food, and sweets, and then spend billions of dollars more on diet food, weight loss programs, and medical care for a host of illnesses such as heart disease and high blood pressure that are often related to improper diet.

Information on the relationship between diet and modern western diseases such as cancer, stroke, and heart attacks has been well researched and widely available to the public for many years; yet doctors rarely advise patients on the role of proper nutrition in the promotion and maintenance of good health. Patients often do not take responsibility to seek out information themselves, tending rather to rely only on chemicals called medicine.

Food Addictions and Eating Disorders

Food builds the body's substance and fuels the body's activities. No matter what the other circumstances of our lives happen to be, most of us in this

ı choose what, when, and how we eat. That there is this
derstanding eating disorders such as anorexia, bulimia, or
ıt genetic. These are addictive behaviors that focus on food
but are not really about food. They are about choice and control and emptiness.

Anorexia (prolonged loss of appetite and refusal to eat) and bulimia (in-
take of large amounts of food followed by purging) are flip sides of the same
coin. These are eating disorders triggered by a terrible psychological loss or
trauma, when one feels trapped or out of control of one's life. By controlling
what or how one eats, there is, perhaps the sense that one is regaining control
over one's life. By undereating, the body is returned to a sexless, childlike
form, and conflicts related to sex are avoided. By overeating, one provides
oneself with a barrier of fat as protection against a terrifying world in which
choices seem very limited. It is interesting to note that there is a high percentage of overweight people in many of the helping professions that deal with
the more difficult personal and social problems.

When the natural relationship between good nutrition and good health is
broken, when food is used as a whip, a lure, a reward, or a punishment, then
it becomes just one more violating behavior. When I was a little girl, I was
coerced and punished by being denied food for days at a time and humiliated
by being served plates of cold food left over from days before. For years I
dreaded going to the dinner table and the new food torture awaiting me.

Social values reinforce eating disorders and addictive behavior with regard to food. In the big cities, "thin is beautiful," and anorexic (looking like
a starved child) is more beautiful, at least according to all the fashion magazines.

Unfortunately for millions, the eating of sugar, salt, fast foods, soft drinks
and fat is remembered as a satisfying part of childhood and continued as a
means of self-comforting in adulthood, often growing into addiction. The last
report of the President's Commission on Physical Fitness reported that *one-
third* of American children are obese and have high blood pressure, and
almost forty percent have no daily physical education classes in school.[12]
Some children never have enough food to eat or eat only junk food. They
don't know the connection between good food and good health, and, if they
also grow up with violence, they may not live long enough to learn. Survivors
of childhood violence often have a hard time accepting their bodies. They
often feel compelled to perpetrate on themselves the abuse that once came
from others. This is the dilemma of violence internalized.

Overcoming food addictions or destructive behavior in relation to food
means addressing issues of control and experiences of abuse or violation
experienced in childhood, setting personal boundaries, and developing a
sense of self-worth. It also means becoming willing to accept and care for
one's own body, developing a realistic self-image, and taking responsibility

for making whatever changes are in one's best interests. Learning self-care after years of bodily abuse by self and others is a challenge.

———————

Food growers are beginning to understand that we cannot continue to poison the earth and water with chemicals if we want to provide enough food for the earth's peoples. The policy of "better, quicker, more" that led to the excessive use of chemicals in agriculture has resulted in chemicals soaking through our soils and poisoning underground water sources to a depth of over fifty feet in some places. Many residents of farm areas can no longer use their well water and must buy bottled water instead. After heavy rains or in the course of irrigation, chemical herbicides, pesticides, and fertilizers run off into streams that then flow into lakes or bays or oceans, killing aquatic grasses, crabs, oysters, clams, and raising to toxic levels the amount of poisonous substances in both fresh and salt water fish.

In 1962, Rachel Carson's book, *Silent Spring*, on exactly this subject, resulted in the banning of DDT and other chemicals—but not before DDT had saturated our food, water, and air. New studies link increased levels of DDT (banned thirty years ago) to breast cancer in women.[13]

We know the facts, and the facts have told us that certain practices and policies are hazardous to health, land, water, fish, livestock, and plants. Why then do such practices and policies continue? This is not rational or life-affirming behavior. It is violent, dysfunctional behavior that is commonplace at least in part because so few are willing to call it dysfunctional and violent.

Sex and Love Addictions

————•————

Sex is the means by which humankind regenerates. It is also the means by which we are able to express intimacy, trust, caring, sensuality, and spirituality through relationship with another.

Love can take the form of protectiveness for a child, a sense of connection to family and community members, and intimacy with a sexual partner. Love is a learned behavior. We first experience it as contact with our birth mother's body, through her eyes, voice, heartbeat, breasts, hands, laughter, song, kiss, smell, and milk. In this context, love means feelings of safety, protection from the world, trust in another, joyfulness, and other expressions that will develop in the process of reaching maturity. Love, therefore, is a range of feelings and learned behaviors that, when appropriately activated, attach us to other people.

Love is contact—with ourselves, with others, and with Spirit.

So what has gone wrong when we speak of addictive sex and "love" addiction?

When love is not part of the childhood experience, when love is withheld or used only as a reward, the child's natural need and desire for love goes underground only to resurface in later years as inappropriate, addictive, or antisocial behaviors.

When violence is a part of a relationship, real love cannot develop. When sex is imposed on a child too early and against his or her will, or without the child being able to decide whether or not they want to participate, then sex becomes an act of violence, of terrorism.

When sex is portrayed as filthy, immoral, sinful, or forbidden, a child will reject and repress normal feelings about his or her developing body and sexuality, only to have those feelings attempt to spring forth years later, resulting in compulsive acts of perversion or violence against others.

When sex and love are separated from one another and sex is used to fill up the emptiness, to numb oneself against feelings, or as a mood changer, then the addictive process has begun. I've heard the sex addict defined as a person who displays maximum attention with minimum intention. The sex addict will do whatever has to be done to engage a partner for sex, without a thought to further contact once the goal is achieved. Sex addicts always keep a supply of partners, so that there is never the risk of being without.

Their focus is on having sex and having it frequently, and on little else. Even when a sex addict is in a long-term relationship, they will keep other sexual partners stashed away in the wings.

Addicts will go to any lengths to protect their supply. Sex addicts use sex as other addicts use drugs or alcohol, so for them, sex has to be in constant supply. If partners are not available, they resort to masturbation. Often, both sexual partners and masturbation are employed to insure the addict of constant sexual stimulus, sometimes without regard to health or safety, appropriate surroundings, or personal reputation. Sex addiction endangers the health of thousands, as it can lead to the transmission of AIDS and venereal diseases. Sex addicts can be found in all walks of life, among religious leaders, politicians, university professors, law enforcement officers, factory workers, etc.

For love addicts, it is the feeling of "being in love" with another that acts as the drug or mood changer, that gives them their "high." Life without this feeling is not worth living, at least from their point of view. Whether the love object is actually participating in the relationship or not is of less importance to the love addict then his or her fantasy, and the allure of the fantasy often precludes all possibility of a real relationship. In extreme cases, love addiction becomes obsession, sometimes resulting in the stalking of and assaults on private individuals, public figures, and even murder.

Many sexual abuse survivors learn a lot about sex much too young. They then find it difficult in adulthood to know how and when to set boundaries, for, when they were children, they were not allowed to say no, nor were they allowed to leave a destructive situation.

Some survivors prefer having sex with strangers and keeping feelings of love only for platonic friends, for combining sex and friendship only evokes feelings of vulnerability and anxiety.

Because these behaviors and the fears behind them are usually not talked about, many people do not realize they result from childhood trauma and may constitute addictions. Without recognition and treatment, addictive behaviors tend to escalate. Many sex and love addicts jeopardize marriages, jobs, social position, relationships with children and other family members, and even their own health without once considering giving up the addiction. Sex and love addictions plague not only private lives of individuals, but threaten public safety through the activities of peeping toms, flashers, mooners, pedophiles, pornographers, sado-masochists, rapists, serial killers, kidnappers, and sexual harassers.

Physical and/or sexual abuse has been the experience of all serial killers whose childhood histories are known. A serial killer evidences an extreme form of addiction, using sex and violence to reenact his past and symbolically annihilate its demons over and over again.

The profile of serial killers is almost as frightening as their behavior. Serial killers are almost always white, middle class males under thirty-five years old. They are rarely married, often described as quiet "loners," and only sporadically employed. All serial killers do violence to their victims beyond simple murder. They torture their victims. They look for a particular set of characteristics in their victims, a stereotype, whether male or female, and, at least in their minds, kill the same person over and over again. The killing usually starts in childhood or adolescence, often with animals, and does not stop until they are caught or have killed themselves.

Why is it necessary to vent so much rage over and over again? What experiences lie behind the serial killer's need to torture and annihilate? What trauma happened to these men when they were innocent children? Who did hurtful things to them? Had they been witness to the torture of others?

Without asking and exploring such questions about serial killers, we lose the opportunity of learning how to prevent the repetition of their hideous acts. Without facing the answers to those questions, we as a society doom ourselves to a life of escalating violence.

FBI agents describe some serial killers as charming men unlikely to provoke suspicion.[14] John Wayne Gary, executed in 1994, was a contractor and fast-food restaurant manager who killed thirty-three young men and boys, burying them in his home in Des Plaines, Illinois. Ted Bundy, executed in 1989, was linked to the murder of thirty-six young women. He had had a job answering calls to a suicide hotline and had gone to law school. Wayne Williams was a free-lance photographer, convicted of killing two of twenty-nine young Atlanta blacks reported missing during a two-year period. Jeffrey Dahmer was convicted of killing fifteen young men of color in Milwaukee, Wisconsin. Dahmer talked about keeping the victims' bodies (usually as parts) so he wouldn't feel abandoned. (Fear of abandonment, of losing mother and being defenseless in the world, is a primary fear in childhood.) Abandonment in childhood is total emptiness and a threat to survival.

These were all young men, personable, intelligent, and nice-looking. All started killing at an early age, Dahmer and Bundy probably as teenagers, though that has not been verified.

Recently, a ten-year-old boy was charged with rape, child molestation, and assault with a knife. His victims were two boys, aged five and eight, and a four-year-old girl. An investigator for the police department in a small town near Portland, Oregon, filed reports on three other cases involving this same child, who may have attacked as many as twelve children in a six-month period.[15] Nothing is reported about this child's background or family life.

But ten-year-old children do not just wake up one morning and start raping and terrorizing other children. Violence is learned behavior. *Something violent happened to that little boy before he became violent.* We have to ask what happened and be willing to hear the answer.

It is likely that most adults suffering from sex and love addictions were physically, sexually, and/or emotionally abused as children. According to the National Committee for the Prevention of Child Abuse, statistics on sexual abuse in the United States indicate that one in every four women is sexually abused before the age of eighteen and one in every eight men is sexually abused before they reach adulthood.

For a great number of people, the damage in childhood was so profound that they will not be able to turn their lives around by themselves. They need many years of therapeutic intervention. Without such help, they may become sociopaths, terrorists, serial killers, pedophiles, or child abusers, many of whom, according to professionals, cannot be rehabilitated! Whether or not that is true, we must uncover the real causes of these behaviors, remembering that once these criminals were innocent children.

The rise in the number of young teenagers engaging in sexual intercourse is, I believe, an example of the national addictions to love and sex, although not currently framed in those terms. Teen sex is a reflection of our consumer values and behaviors as glorified in the media and of the attitudes of adults who look upon their children merely as objects to possess.

Currently, one million teenagers become pregnant each year.[16] Two-thirds of the teenagers who give birth are single. Only one in ten of black teens giving birth is married. When asked why they have babies, most reply that they are looking for LOVE. They are seeking the love they cannot find in their homes, from their families, or in society. The symptom is the rise in teenage pregnancies; the disease is the unavailability of love, self-esteem, empowerment, and feelings of belonging in everyday life, particularly in families of violence.

Young male teenagers often assume a "hit and run" attitude toward sex, impregnating as many girls as possible to prove their manhood, and increase their standing among their peers. To ask young people to "just say no" to sex without giving them adequate education as to why is unrealistic, even cruel. Without adequate information, unless the child has the benefit of a deeply loving and highly ethical family, he or she most likely will be overwhelmed by the many hazards and temptations facing young people on a daily basis.

One-fourth of all girls and one-third of boys are sexually active by the age of fifteen. By the age of seventeen, fifty percent of all girls and sixty-six percent of all boys are sexually active. Half of these children receive no education about AIDS. A Massachusetts study in 1991 found that one in forty-six young people checked for AIDS tested positive.[17]

In the name of "protecting" children from premature sexual encounters, authorities, parents, and religious leaders are keeping them in the dark, thus risking the lives of an entire generation of youth to sexually transmitted diseases and the killer AIDS. The fact that condoms can reduce the risk of AIDS by ninety percent and unwanted pregnancy by approximately the same figure[18] gets lost in the rhetoric of "old-fashioned family values." In this instance, renaming the problem is essential.

At present only about twenty-five percent of sexually active high school seniors say they always use condoms. Insult is added to injury when thirty-four percent of college males say they have lied to potential sex partners about using a condom. Not surprisingly, sixty-three percent of venereal disease cases occur in men and women under twenty-five years old.[19]

Here, too, renaming the problem is important. Most discussion on teenage pregnancy focuses on the female. Where are the fathers? Where are the child support payments? Where are the responsible legislators? Why is it that the media, social services, courts and other law enforcement institutions, medical community, and society at large still define the problem only in terms of the mother, the female? Where is acknowledgement of shared responsibility for co-creation from initial sexual encounter to conception to parenthood?

We must seek to redefine this issue in terms of responsibility shared by both men and women, or risk an ever-growing number of young victims in the future.

Addictions to Spending and Gambling

The United States government has a spending addiction. So do millions of its ordinary citizens.

Throughout most of history, money as we know it today did not exist. Instead, people bartered, exchanging goods, services, property, and sometimes other people. In pre-historic times, exchange systems were communal and designed for the overall well-being of the community.

While many empires made use of coinage, it was not until the Europeans explored the Americas in the sixteenth and seventeenth centuries that vast amounts of gold and silver coins were put into circulation on the European continent, creating a newly rich merchant class. This meant the end of the old feudal order whereby serfs were tied to regional landowners whose power and status were passed down through the bloodline.

Money became so plentiful that systems for handling money were developed. Those who had plenty were able to lend it to others for a fee, what is now called *interest*. Early Christians called money lending for interest *usury* and prohibited its practice. (In Islamic cultures money lending is still banned.) Only Jewish money lenders were permitted to charge interest (e.g., Shylock in Shakespeare's *Merchant of Venice*), creating from their profits powerful banks and merchant city-states, like Venice, Italy.

But for people living outside the cities, money played only a secondary role. Until the end of World War II, most of the population in the United States lived in the countryside, in small towns, and on farms. With the end of the war, the industries that had gone into action to produce wartime machinery and weapons were turned to the production of consumer goods, cars, and appliances. Advertising encouraged everyone to *buy*.

America became a consumer-driven economy almost overnight. Industry extended credit. Merchants extended credit. The banks extended a new kind of credit in the form of plastic cards. All that credit created a frenzied buying spree that created so much debt, now no one knows how to repay it.

Spending became a virtue. People everywhere rushed to get more of everything—houses, cars, appliances, electronic equipment, toys, vacations.

The government, itself addicted to spending, suddenly had to depend on consumer spending for economic expansion, and so encouraged more spending, which resulted in more debt, for individuals and itself. Today, two-thirds of the American economy is dependent on consumer spending.

During the 1980s, government debt went out of control, but since everyone was addicted to spending, no one wanted to face it. Consumerism had been sold to the public as a virtue, so any argument against it was easily defeated. The rising debt, both personal and governmental, was a source of shame, kept a secret or denied, or disguised by terms like *credit*. Spending became linked with self-worth and self-esteem. Previously, saving money had been considered a virtue, but no longer. Shoplifting, petty thievery, and grand larceny increased dramatically. People shopped to distract themselves from relationship problems and any and all other anxieties. Shopping became a drug. To be able to buy nice things could lessen anxiety, make one feel good about oneself, provide some form of security, and temporarily fill that lost, empty feeling brought forward from a childhood in which real needs were ignored or denied.

The consequences of our national addiction to spending are evident in savings and loan failures, bank foreclosures, junk bond fraud, leveraged buyout mergers that have left many U.S. companies insolvent, and insurance companies that have had to go into receivership. These massive financial failures have cost taxpayers billions of dollars and have created anxiety in innocent people who trusted and were deceived.

Meanwhile, leaders urge still more consumer spending in order to keep this false economy afloat. The media gluts the airwaves, newspapers, and magazines with images of glitz and glamour, encouraging spending as a way to solve life's problems. These messages do not go unnoticed. When young people cannot buy the "right" clothes or shoes, some will kill to get them.[20]

Here again, violence is closely linked to addiction. As illustrated by the Survivor's Wheel, destructive and antisocial behaviors arise and multiply when the underlying causes of dysfunction are not addressed. Poverty alone does not explain killing for shoes and jackets.

Closely related to addiction to spending is addiction to gambling, now encouraged by the creation of more and more legal gambling opportunities.[21] Casinos, lotteries, racetracks, poker games, bingo games, and sports competitions mean money, money, money. The addicted gambler bets on anything with anyone. The entertainment industry and the stock market depend on the urge to gamble.

The lure of gambling is the thrill of danger and taking risks, it's the possibility of the big score, the big fix, it's beating the odds and cheating the IRS. Gambling can give the gambler a feeling of power, at least when he's winning; but most gamblers lose most of the time.

As with all other addictions, when the fever hits, all else is left behind and the consequences can be disastrous.

Workaholism

The practices of a workaholic—putting work before self and family, dedicating oneself totally to career, working long hours and weekends—are generally rewarded by employers and society. Workaholics are more tied to job and workplace than they are to anything or anyone else. In the name of "doing their job," these people may neglect personal relationships, parenting responsibilities, even their own health. When work gets the best of one's time, energy, and imagination, when nothing is left over for friends, spouse, lovers, children, or oneself, work is an addiction.

Work addicts are often surprised when friends or family ask for more attention or time. After all, how can one criticize a person who works so hard, provides so well, and is so tired as a result? The work addict will say he or she has "no choice," the time they give to work is the time required to do and to keep a good job. Work addicts rarely have hobbies or take pleasure in recreational activities except those, like golf or tennis games with clients and associates, that are work-related.

Work addicts can be so busy working they miss the process of growth and development in their children. Their children see them as strangers, resent the abandonment, and frequently act out. Today, it is the norm for both parents to work and not unusual for children to grow up in single-parent homes. Young people often have no sense of being parented at all. Adults are either too busy at work, too self-involved, or too tired. Peer groups, including gangs, become a logical substitute for families. Susceptible to advertising and fads, frustrated by parental neglect and lack of supervision, these children eventually find themselves in trouble. At this point, the child may finally catch the work addict's attention, but the communication gap from years of neglect may be nearly insurmountable. It is then one hears the parent say, "Where did I go wrong? I gave them everything," or, "How could they do this to me?"

When addiction takes over, basic needs for sleep, proper food, exercise, and freedom to refresh the mind and restore the spirit are ignored. Relationships are fitted in around the work schedule, and, if work takes all the time, then there are no relationships, except on the most casual and catch-as-catch-can basis.

Engaging in work-addicted behavior over a long period of time will numb the addict to feelings, to the condition of the environment, and to the condition of his or her body, health, and/or emotional and spiritual life. Away from work, the person may feel disconnected and at odds. Through addiction, the workaholic has avoided feeling anxiety, emptiness, lack of control, and other emotions that communicate life's realities.

The current high level of unemployment is particularly hard on work addicts. Of course, it is difficult for anyone to be without work and a means of sustaining self and family, but for the work addict it is a crisis accompanied by withdrawal symptoms and extreme anxiety. For them, it is not just the loss of a paycheck, it is the loss of self-worth, lifestyle, and their "fix." Since they never developed a life apart from work, without a job they are faced with total emptiness—exactly what they sought so diligently to avoid.

The effects of work addiction can be read in the following statistics:

- Worker's compensation claims related to stress tripled during the first half of the 1980s;
- More fatal heart attacks occur at 9am on Monday than at any other time;
- The number of people showing up at sleep disorder clinics has skyrocketed in the last decade.
- A "sleep deficit" is prevalent among Americans, indicating that they are sleeping sixty to ninety minutes less than is necessary for optimum health and performance.[22]

To people brought up in families in which their own needs came after everyone else's or not at all, the abuses of dysfunctional, abusive job structures are hardly noticeable. If there was also disrespect and violence in their families, these people will be vulnerable to manipulation, deception, and other forms of revictimization in the workplace. If they become managers or executives, they are likely to administer in the authoritarian manner they learned from their parents, creating an atmosphere at work that encourages disrespectful, manipulative, power-based behavior and punishes any deviations.

For some, this similarity of the workplace to their childhood experience, no matter how traumatic, actually feels safe, because all factors are known and all behaviors are more or less predictable. In such an environment, one never has to grow up. When jobs did offer security, the worker was taken care of in return for his unconditional loyalty; but that pleasant scenario is impossible in today's uncertain job market.

Some survivors tend to resist cooperative ventures because they have trouble trusting others. They did not experience being treated with respect and consideration in childhood and do not expect it in adulthood. These people cannot tolerate working under too much structure or authority. Preferring to work on their own, they become artists, craftspeople, technicians, entrepreneurs, independent consultants, and contractors.

My early years were just too punishing, too violent, too sadistic, too damaging to my self-esteem for me to flourish in a corporate environment. It has taken me many years to figure out how and where I fit best and not to judge myself a failure or a misfit because working in the "mainstream" feels toxic to my spirit.

Today all jobs are scarce and good jobs are precious. Now it will be tempting to exploit these conditions, to scapegoat employees, to decrease benefits, to demand longer hours for the same wage, to encourage workaholism. This is a growing challenge we face.

Unless they have begun to deal with their past, people who come from backgrounds of family violence tend not to question the rules by which they live and work. The message takes many forms but is always the same: our only hope of stopping present-day abuses is to examine the abuses of the past.

Addiction to Exercise

The human body is meant to be active. We feel better and perform more effectively when we get a regular amount of exercise. Exercise keeps us trim, fit, and healthy. Exercise triggers the body's built-in reward system by releasing endorphines that produce a feeling of exhilaration, sometimes called "joggers high." While millions of Americans, including children, have become couch potatoes, others incur serious injury from improper or excessive exercise. Injury and pain are clues as to whether the line has been crossed from healthy fitness to compulsive behavior. The use of steroids for increased performance is a good example of the latter.

When exercise is used to replace social interaction and relationships, it may be more addiction than choice. Are you pursuing fitness, or violating your body? Have you become obsessed, so that you exercise more and more hours every day and can no longer function normally without doing so?

The past one hundred years have brought so many technological advancements and conveniences that substantially less physical effort is now required for everyday life. That means decreased blood circulation and muscle stretching, less efficient metabolism of food, and less stress reduction through physical activity. Exercise today is an activity one has to organize; it is no longer an integral part of living.

Children's team sports, such as Little League, Pop Warner football, and competitive swimming and tennis can become a means of abuse by parents who exploit their children's skills and successes for their own ego gratification. Enjoyment, exercise, building team skills, and the child's emotional and physical well-being become unimportant, and winning is everything.

Professional sports have become obsessive, big money pursuits in which excellence, stardom, and violence are intertwined. Recently, there have been outbreaks of spectator violence at soccer, hockey, and football games. Even traditionally non-violent sports are no longer so. Tennis and figure-skating stars have been intentionally injured to increase their competitors' chances for success. Winning is everything. Violence is the means of choice for conflict resolution and self-fulfillment.

The challenge is balance: physical, emotional, and psychological balance.

Exercise, when not integrated into a life in a natural and balanced way, can easily become addiction or yet another means for the expression of violence.

Religion

Religion is undoubtedly the most difficult addiction to discuss openly. Just raising the subject evokes fears, memories of family beliefs and training, social judgments, and, worst of all, hatred and intolerance toward those whose beliefs are different.

All three major western religions (Judaism, Christianity, and Islam) have used their teachings to gain authority over followers, to create wars, and to suppress belief in any religion other than theirs. All three have treated women as less than men. Under all three banners, abusive and violent cults have flourished in the name of family, God, and country.

Religion and spirituality are vitally important elements in all cultures. Neither are intrinsically abusive. It is the misuse of power by religions and spiritual leaders that becomes addictive and leads to abuses. And it is the blind trust of those leaders by their followers that perpetuates the abuse.

Religious authority rarely permits questioning by followers, just as abusive and violent parents do not allow their authority to be questioned. The experience of arbitrary parental authority in early family life may make people more vulnerable to cults or charismatic leaders that manipulate followers for personal power and wealth. Cults can become a form of religious addiction, a means by which people recreate their family of origin: followers become the "children" and the cult leader becomes the parent who makes the rules, decides the punishments, and extorts unconditional love, loyalty, and obedience.

Lately, self-help groups have begun forming specifically to address religious addiction and abuse. Victims of abuse by clergy are joining forces to prosecute their abusers, even after decades have passed. These confrontations with religious authority require courage from the individual and the support of the community.

Much sexual abuse has been perpetrated with religious overtones, with threats of hell and damnation. Ritual (satanic) abuse is conducted through the black mass or other dark magical/religious rites intended to increase the subjugation of both victim and participants. Since millions have been taught from childhood not to question religious authority or doctrine, ritual abuse survivors have a very difficult time being believed when they attempt to get help. Denial blocks their way when they detail how religion or religious leaders have been perverted.

The exploitation of religion for political purposes is another form of abuse of power whose roots may lie in childhood experience. The United States Constitution guarantees separation of church and state precisely because our founding fathers knew firsthand the oppression of state-mandated religious practice and how it can lead to violence (i.e., the Inquisition). They were determined to create a different system based on individual human rights and personal freedom.

During the past decade, this principle has been seriously challenged. Religious groups have attempted to influence government policy against those with different beliefs. In some cases, fanatic (addictive) adherence to religious beliefs has led to violence: a pro-life advocate shot a doctor who worked in a family planning clinic; Moslem fundamentalists bombed the World Trade Center in New York City. Intolerance inevitably leads to violence, as history has proven generation after generation.

Religion becomes both a violation of others' rights and a form of addiction under the following circumstances:
- When it is forced, rather than voluntary;
- When it abuses trust for personal gratification;
- When it misuses power to exploit others;
- When it seeks to force behaviors on others through political manipulation;
- When it uses any form of violence (i.e., "end justifies means") against others of different belief systems;
- When it isolates its followers from the rest of the world in order to remain "pure";
- When it is a compulsive escape from everyday reality and used to justify abusive behavior toward family, friends, and self.

Interpersonal Behavior

CHAPTER 4

Interpersonal Behavior

Our relationships with friends, family, lovers, spouse, children, co-workers are directly linked to our experiences early in life. How we were treated as children, even before we started school, largely determines how we will treat others.

"As within, so without; as above, so below." The meaning of this aphorism is that the inner and outer worlds mirror one another. This wisdom becomes particularly clear in relationships.

It is through the mirror of our relationships with others that we begin to understand ourselves. Relationship difficulties are often the catalyst that brings people into therapy or support groups. The quality of one's relationships is a key factor in assessing one's growth, maturity, and healthiness. We see who we are by whom we choose to be with and how they treat us.

It is also in relationships with others that violence, learned in childhood and often deeply buried from memory, resurfaces in many different forms. While others their age are making professional and social progress, people raised in violent families often find themselves in their thirties and forties having to re-evaluate their childhood experiences just in order to survive.

The Survivor's Wheel illustrates how relationships mirror the original childhood trauma, while simultaneously serving as coping mechanisms to assuage old pain. Thus past and present meet in relationships. When the encounter is approached with awareness, healing from past trauma can be accomplished.

Violence takes many forms. It is not limited to the physical abuse of children or the battering of a spouse.

Psychological violence also can leave deep scars. Humiliation, shaming, name calling, raging, and terrorizing are all forms of non-physical violence that violate by attacking vulnerabilities, by devouring self-esteem, and by disrespecting and devaluing the dignity of another. Furthermore, these violating behaviors provoke legitimate reactions of anger, hatred, rage, and violence in their victims, thus perpetuating the problem.

In her book, *Facing Co-Dependence*, Pia Melody depicts the child as being *naturally* valuable, vulnerable, imperfect, dependent, and immature. In a healthy atmosphere, these characteristics will be encouraged to mature and transform into those of adulthood. When a child is treated as valuable, self-esteem from *within* can emerge. When a child is allowed to be vulnerable in conditions of safety and respect, a sense of healthy boundaries develops. When imperfection is accepted and not punished or shamed, a spiritual life can be embraced. When dependency needs are met, the child can learn how to form interdependent alliances and to get his/her needs met responsibly. When a child's immaturity is accepted and embraced, he or she can develop naturally and appropriately to age.

In violent families, however, the natural characteristics of the child are treated as flaws, faults, or fundamental damage deserving of punishment. Every normal trait is used *against* the child, who is made to feel shame and guilt and grows up feeling doomed to failure.

Family violence teaches children that they are worthless, unwanted, and deserving of neglect, beating, rape, and being thrown into the streets to survive however they can. Their vulnerability is not protected. They are exploited and manipulated to meet the needs of their parents. Their imperfections are ridiculed. Their dependency meets with abandonment, guilting, shaming, or is totally ignored. Their immaturity is not allowed its natural duration, as they are made into sexual partners, surrogate parents to their own parents, addiction procurers, and alter egos.

As these children reach adolescence and adulthood, they try to assume the characteristics of maturity without any real knowledge or experience of them as a foundation. One day they are children and the next day they are sexual partners or drug dealers, carrying guns and killing people. Survivors are faced with the unenviable, painful, and difficult task of developing in adulthood skills and experiences that are normally learned in childhood—that is, if they live long enough to become adults.

Few Friends

Mark Twain wrote: "The holy passion of friendship is of so sweet and steady and loyal and enduring a nature that it will last through a whole lifetime, if not asked to lend money."[1]

Leaving the issue of money aside, friendship is both a personal skill and a gift from others. Friends see us through crisis, through professional success and failure, through romances, marriages, and illnesses—if we have friends.

For people who grow up with violence, the issue of friendship is a crucial one, because most do not have a family they can turn to in either good times or bad. However, survivors of family violence may not know how to choose friends or be a friend to others. They may feel they cannot trust anyone and that they have to "go it alone."

For these people, friendships are crucial as an alternative source of positive support that was never experienced in family relationships. The survivor cannot turn to family members for help or to share joys and successes. "You can choose your friends, even if you can't choose your family," the old saying goes. Friends may take on the role of sister, brother, mother, father, or even of a child.

Friendship requires mutual trust. It is founded in sharing values and respect.

We first learn these qualities by being with someone we can trust, rely on, and share with, someone who also trusts and shares with us. As we grow, we experiment with others and develop skills necessary to build and maintain friendships. These qualities include trust, respect for oneself, and respect for others, even if they are very different.

In the environment of family violence, children learn disrespect and mistrust and that adults do not live up to their promises, do not tell the truth, are not available to listen, cannot be trusted with sensitive information, and disrespect personal boundaries.

Violence or the threat of violence used against a small child by a parent, caretaker, or other adult is not trustworthy behavior. Violence is the ultimate lack of respect toward another person, particularly if that person is a defenseless infant or child.

Seeing violence used as a primary means of resolving arguments or interpersonal disputes teaches a child that violence is acceptable and may be used to get one's own way. It teaches disrespect for the lives and bodies of others. It teaches fear and hatred. These are the essential elements of terrorism.

Distrust is the only reasonable response to survive family violence. Rather than saying what he/she wants or feels with trust that it will be heard, the child soon learns to manipulate and connive in order to get what he/she needs from adults. But although lying is, in the short run, more believable and effective and less troublesome than telling the truth, in the long run, it causes major problems in relationships.

If one cannot be trusted, one cannot have real friends or real relationships of any kind as an adult. To the survivor who cannot tell the truth, who cannot be trusted or trust, other people become merely a means to an end. While such relationships are very common these days, they are also unsatisfying and filled with unhappiness.

Friendship is about sharing—sharing toys, food, fun, sports, games, ideas, tears, triumphs, upsets, confidences, and possessions. Sharing is learned behavior based on mutual agreement and trust. Without mutual agreement, sharing becomes theft, which then leads to conflict.

In trusting another, one feels assured that one will not be taken advantage of, that one can affirm one's rights and retrieve one's possessions without the need for obstruction, seduction, manipulation, or violent action from either party. Trust permits negotiation and conflict resolution. It is not common in today's social interactions.

When a child grows up in a violent household, other kids will not be invited over. Opportunities for friendships to evolve and deepen become limited and compartmentalized.

Boundaries define where one person ends and the other person begins and are necessary for healthy friendships. As infants, we experience no boundaries because we are so attached to and dependant on the mother/caregiver. As we grow, we must separate our identity from that of our parent(s). Having a sense of that separation or boundary means giving up those early feelings of total union, of being merged with or of disappearing into another. It means you know you are separate from the other, that each of you has needs and rights that may be similar but may also be very different. Boundaries are a means of deciding when to say yes and when to say no, when to hold one's ground on behalf of one's own needs as opposed to the needs of another. Boundaries are an expression of personal responsibility. Boundaries are healthy.

Survivors of family violence, however, were never allowed to choose for themselves, never allowed to say no without experiencing disastrous repercussions. Survivors of family violence grow up with no boundaries.

In any relationship, they often feel overwhelmed, that they have disappeared as a separate individual and have been absorbed in the identity of another, just as they were as children. Being "taken over" by someone else, feeling controlled, fearful, humiliated in their presence, is a most unpleasant experience.

When one is abused or mistreated as a child, one suffers profound disrespect to body, mind, and spirit. If the abuse continues over months and years, as is true for most survivors, the child becomes conditioned to feeling worthless as a separate human being.

This is the terrible void handguns and automatic weapons are filling. Increasing numbers of people believe that having a handgun will assure them the "respect" they were never given otherwise. Thus a natural desire, long thwarted, becomes distorted, and guns become the purveyors of self-esteem, putting all of America at risk.

Some survivors prefer to avoid close personal relationships rather than risk feeling annihilated all over again. Others realize they don't have the necessary skills for being or having a friend. Many of these become loners, confirmed bachelors, or maiden aunts, while others may become "stalkers," mass murderers, pedophiles—all isolated and lonely, and some dangerous. How often have we heard or read the suspect described as "a quiet person, who kept to himself, and didn't seem to have any friends." It is a description so common as to make up a profile.

Even if all other factors of a person's life appear normal, not having friends is a strong indication of being a survivor.

Non-criminal survivors, when they face times of deep stress, become dangerous to themselves rather than to others, developing physical and emotional illnesses, phobias, and antisocial behaviors, sometimes becoming homeless or dying in isolation.

Our evolutionary pattern as a species has been to live in groups, communally. Companionship and friendship are expressions of the natural way of life of our species. Social contact, researchers are discovering, may also encourage the production of protective hormones that help to promote health and prevent disease. For example, research indicates that heart attack victims living alone are twice as likely to suffer another attack within six months as those living with another or others.[2]

Dr. James House of the University of Michigan believes isolation is a major health risk, as "significant to mortality rates as smoking, high blood pressure, high cholesterol, obesity and lack of physical exercise."[3] Most at risk are those who have no one with whom to share feelings or who have close contact with other people less than once a week.

Some survivors of violent, despotic, addictive, and neglectful families of origin do form bonds of friendship, but the nature of those bonds is affected by the survivor's childhood experience.

Some survivors may choose friends who make them feel angry or bad about themselves on a regular basis, or they may choose others with whom they can share addictive or anti-social behaviors. Such relationships are most likely replays of abusive family relationships, a dance from the past to which at least they know all the steps. They often feel betrayed, as though their trust and caring were stolen from them. This pattern can lead to bitterness and an unwillingness to try relationships of any kind again, a downward spiral into loneliness and dis-ease of spirit, if not of body and mind.

Survivors of abusive or highly authoritarian families or of environments in which a parent was chronically ill, alcoholic, or drug-addicted tend to need a lot of control, for they want to avoid at all costs a repetition of the chaos of their childhoods. It is an ironical truth that life usually calms down and becomes more satisfying only when one surrenders the unhealthy desire to control others' behavior; but this is an act of great trust and faith, an act not easy for most survivors.

Without friends, life can become very limited and overly self-absorbed. One can lose a sense of one's place in the context of the whole of humanity.

Friendship means caring, and most survivors did not know much caring or kindness as children. At first, experiencing caring and kindness outside the family setting may feel frightening and dangerous, or strange at the very least; but survivors must learn what such qualities look and feel like in order to make them a part of their lives.

The greatest danger in having few friends is the loss of mirroring and feedback that friendship can provide. Without such feedback about one's choices, goals, actions, and state of being, one can get very far off track without being aware of it.

Friendships provide affirmation, connection, and balance. Healthy friendships are life sustaining.

Lack of Intimacy

Intimacy should be the first experience in one's life. If it is not, if mother and child do not bond, then intimacy may become something the survivor fears and avoids.

True intimacy requires the highest level of trust between two people.

Intimacy means being vulnerable while trusting that one is safe and accepted, fully seen and heard by another human being.

As one grows to adulthood, the possibilities of intimacy expand beyond the bond between parent and child to include social intimacy (sharing of experience), sexual intimacy (sharing of touch, intercourse), emotional intimacy (sharing of feelings), intellectual intimacy (sharing of ideas), artistic intimacy (sharing of creativity), and spiritual intimacy (sharing of the quest for essential understanding).

Most survivors believe in their hearts that "if you ever really got to know me, you'd dislike me/hate me and leave me." The behavior of their parent(s) taught them so, sometimes before they were able to speak, before they had words to express their thoughts and feelings about the treatment they were receiving. Without such possibilities of expression, the abusive, abandoning, or rejecting behaviors and attitudes of the parents were only more easily internalized. As a consequence, to a survivor, it would make absolute sense that in order to keep someone close, the last thing to do would be to strip off the mask and reveal the true self.

Of course, jobs, friendships, marriages, and parenting can be undertaken without true intimacy; but there is at some point at least a subliminal recognition that something is wrong, something is missing.

Without early bonding, survivors cannot develop a sense of safety in the world, a sense of competence in coping with setbacks, a feeling of compassion for others. Dr. Ken Magid, in his book *High Risk*, describes a scale of relative bonding capacities, from no-bonding to high-bonding potential, as exemplified by Mother Theresa. Successful early bonding fosters traits that we consider valuable in both private relationships and society at large, while the lack of such bonds often results in sociopaths and psychopaths.

The failure of an intimate relationship is the most frequent motivation for people to seek help with their personal difficulties for the first time. When accompanied by willingness to confront those difficulties honestly, this can lead to a major step forward toward freeing the survivor from a history of automatic and self-defeating behaviors. Ironically, intimacy is often the last reward of the recovery process, as much other work must be done first, and mostly alone, before true intimacy can be achieved.

Survivors must learn to allow themselves to be vulnerable, to admit mistakes, to tell the truth, to express feelings, to expose doubt or shyness or lack of knowledge. Being vulnerable can be seen by survivors as handing the enemy the ammunition with which to kill them; for, as children, their imperfections and lack of maturity—natural characteristics of their age—had been twisted into faults and causes for blame, humiliation, and punishment.

But the experience of connection to another human, of being loved, respected, cared for, seen, heard, accepted, acknowledged, and of trusting and being trusted is one of the most essential to human life. Intimacy is the foundation for compassion, and compassion for others and for self is the basis of a healthily functioning society.

Intimacy allows that no one is quite perfect, and yet each can be loved, loving, and valuable. With true intimacy, no one need have all the answers, all the control, or all the attention. Intimacy fosters gentleness and permits passion, but not the violent passion of anger or rage.

True intimacy is a powerful bulwark against the violence and terror plaguing our times.

"as ye sow . . . so shall ye reap . . ."

My adoptive mother married once when I was three-and-one-half and once when I was sixteen years old. Both marriages ended after three years, the first by divorce and the second with the death of my stepfather. In each case, she married a man I'd not met, a man who simply appeared one day as her husband and whom I was then instructed to call Daddy. Before my birth and adoption, she had been married and divorced twice, each of these marriages lasting three years each as well. Thus she was a single woman and a single parent most of her adult life.

Divorce was so common among the families I knew as a child, so many of my friends came from what were then called "broken homes," that we used to joke about it:

1st Kid:"Heard your mom got married again. How do you like your new stepfather?"

2nd Kid:"Oh, he's all right, I guess."

3rd Kid:"Yeah, he's not too bad. We had him last year."

There was little continuity in male/female relationships. People came and went without explanation. No one thought it important enough to discuss these changes with their children. In fact, when a parent ended a relationship, we were often cautioned not to speak of it again. We were denied the opportunity to grieve the loss of a person we had come to care about. Our feelings, thoughts, and needs in relation to our own families were totally ignored, as though they didn't exist.

As a result, I had no way of learning how to enter into or leave a relationship. In fact, I may not have understood that there was any process at all. These things just seemed to happen, as if by magic. When a relationship became too unpleasant or intrusive, too scary and close, I would just walk away, usually without explanation. This was the only way I knew. There were no goodbyes, no closure. Everything was instant, like turning off a light switch.

The message from my childhood experiences with adults came through loud and clear: "Don't become close to anyone, or you will be betrayed and abandoned."

Children learn about life by watching their parents' actions, even more than by listening to their words. Generally, we tend to imitate what we see more than what we hear, if the two are in contradiction. It may take years of adulthood to sort out those behaviors internalized by observing and experiencing the behaviors of their parents, despite the fact that most survivors are adamant about wanting to be anything but like their parents.

Like my mother, I also married several times. My first marriage, at the age twenty-six, lasted only two years, after which I became very ill. My second marriage began when I was thirty-six and ended with divorce nine years later. During that marriage, I nearly died from a massive stroke.

At fifty-one, I remarried a third time. I have been married a total of about fourteen years, so I, too, have been single most of my life. Thankfully, I knew I was too young or too angry and unskilled in relationships to care properly for children and chose not to have any of my own.

Statistics tell us that American marriages end in divorce at almost twice the rate of any other industrialized country;[4] but statistics cannot begin to convey the anger, bitterness, disruption, hardship, and anguish of loss faced by all parties to the divorce. Many children today will grow up with more than one step-family, as both biological parents marry several times. Many children will live for extended periods with a single and/or estranged parent and with conflict over visiting rights or child support payments.

Psychologist Barbara Hayes has studied the effects of divorce on child development. She has constructed a chart utilizing the work of developmental psychologist Erik Ericson Benjamin Wolman, Gerald Weeks, and Bonnie Robson to show the stages of normal child development and how divorce negatively efffects that development. The chart (on the following page) clearly illustrates how the trauma of divorce impacts a child, creating fears and survivor behaviors instead of normal development:[5]

Birth to 2 years: Normally, the child develops trust and hope. However, if the parents divorce during this stage, the trauma instills mistrust. Later problems include food and sleep disorders.

2 to 3 years: The child normally develops a sense of self. The trauma of divorce can lead instead to a sense of shame and self-doubt, resulting in fears of abandonment and death, as well as other fears that may become phobias.

3 to 5 years: The child should develop initiative and a sense of purpose and learns sharing and social awareness. The trauma of divorce confuses development of internal controls and can trigger guilt feelings. The child develops sexual fears and the fear of being left alone, and angry feelings develop.

5 to 10 years: The child normally develops higher learning capacity, competence, and friendships. Trauma hampers the ability to go into the world

with a feeling of self-worth. Feelings of inferiority develop instead of confidence. The child fears rejection, failure, physical danger, and has nightmares.

10 to 15 years: The child should further develop self-worth, begin to join groups and to learn fidelity. With trauma, the child begins to "act out" and to express anger, frustration, heightened dependency on others, and confusion of sex roles. Anxiety replaces fear. Psychosexual identity is impaired.

15 to adult: If the previous developmental stages have been adequately experienced and integrated, then a sense of self matures enough to participate in love, intimacy, and a sense of mutuality with other adults. If the previous developmental processes have been interrupted or distorted by trauma, then the developing adult will likely be dealing with fears, phobia, anxiety, shame, guilt, lack of self-esteem, addiction, and substance abuse—all afflictions common to the survivor of family violence.

Dr. Hayes, as the final entry on the chart, notes that for those traumatized in childhood, "Life and relationships lead to acute anxiety, panic, depression."[6] These reactions create the foundation for relationship failure and divorce, for delinquency and criminal activity, and for a myriad of health-related problems. More positively, they also lead thousands of survivors to seek therapy and counseling.

Of course, not all who grow up victims of divorce, abuse, or neglect get divorced, and not every divorce leads to such life-threatening problems; but all divorce should be viewed as a source of trauma for children. By understanding the impact of divorce on a child's developmental processes, it should be clear that its trauma can induce survivor coping behaviors to take shape very early in life, affecting not only childhood, but also how the person matures into adulthood. When development cannot proceed along normal lines, emotional responses and behaviors become distorted and often self-defeating. What is not learned in childhood will have to be learned in adulthood, if the survivor is fortunate enough to live long enough, and if he or she has the will to heal, to learn, and undo the negatives of past influences in early life.

Probably it is not coincidental that more and more people are choosing to remain single, to live in same sex partnerships, and/or not to produce children. Others go from one failed, violent, disrespectful relationship to another, never understanding their own drives or why nothing seems to work out in their lives. They are without knowledge of the long-term effects on adult behavior of a traumatic childhood in which they witnessed or experienced firsthand powerful, dysfunctional behavior often reinforced by violence.

Marriage for survivors may bring up long buried feelings and memories from childhood that cause anxiety and even panic. These may include a sense

DEVELOPMENT AND DIVORCE—A SKELETAL VIEW			
Approx. Age	**Optimal Normal Development**	**Potential Impact of Divorce**	**Children's Fears**
0–2 years	Earliest awareness of separation. Reciprocity of exchange. Development of trust. Foundation of ability to consolidate strengths for purposeful behavior and capacity to hope.	Mistrust regarding outer experience. Difficulties can appear around sleep, eating, excreting. Behavioral regression.	Loud noises. The unknown or unfamiliar. Overstimulation.
2–3 years	Sense of self. Sense of power. Onset of autonomy, mastery, and willpower.	Security and routine are disrupted. Emergence of doubt. Regressive, negative behavior. Whining. Expressing needs of earlier stage. Foundation of sense of shame and self-doubt.	Anxiety. Strangers, dogs and other animals, the dark, night. Separation, abandonment, death, disappearing.
3–5 years	Development of initiative. Cooperation, mutuality, social awareness. Identification with same sex parent. Underpinnings of sense of direction and sense of purpose.	Confusion in consolidation of self, development of internal controls, conscience, and identification with same sex parent. Forerunner of guilt. Child believes he is responsible for events in his life.	Animals, snakes, strange noises, goblins. Scary movies. Being left alone, dark rooms. Creations of own imagination. Sexual fears. Child's own angry feelings.
5–10 years	Development of cognitive capacities and sense of industry. Underpinnings of competence. Peers and friendships.	Guilt over family rupture impedes ability to venture into world. Sense of inferiority impacts relationships and accomplishments.	Nightmares. Ridicule. disapproval, rejection, failure. Physical danger. Divorce. Parent's well-being, parent's death.
10–15 years	Self-identification begins. Belonging to peer group. Self-worth. Foundation of devotion and fidelity.	Need for stability at home, for home to be backdrop: disrupted by parental blaming, alliances, unhappiness, financial tension. Anger, frustration, fear, heightened dependency. "Acting out" behavior. Confusion of role.	Anxiety replaces fear. Failure, inadequacy. Dependence. Rejection by peer group. Psychosexual identity.
15–21 years 21–30 years	Self-identification continues. Intimacy. Mutuality. If previous stages successfully integrated, love and affiliation.	Intimacy threatens impaired sense of self from previous disruptions. Pseudomutuality, isolation. Addictive behavior. Substance use.	Life and relationships lead to acute anxiety, panic, depression.

of confinement or abandonment or memories of violence in intimate contact buried among yearnings for love and tenderness that were never fulfilled. The survivor may experience feelings of doom or sadness and depression which, in the light of the present, make no sense to him or her or to anyone else and cause feelings of "being different," "never fitting in," "feeling crazy," and "never being understood."

Survivors frequently expect the marriage partner to be nearly clairvoyant, able to anticipate needs before they are spoken—as a caring parent will do for an infant or toddler. The survivor's partner is expected always to take the survivor's side, no matter what the situation. The spouse or partner of the survivor is cast in the role of defender and protector—much the way a caring parent of a young child helps the child begin to negotiate the outside world, providing a sense of protection and safety. The survivor looks to his partner for the missing pieces of parenting that he never received during childhood. Thus the relationship is not between two adults, but rather between a child/ survivor and an adult or, more likely, between two child/survivors who look adult but have no maturity or sense of self, no matter their chronological age.

Survivors usually choose other survivors with whom to have relationships, recognizing one another almost instantly, as if by an invisible, built-in antenna. Survivors share a knowledge of how to live with long-term abuse, magical thinking, addiction, and dysfunction. Other ways of being in the world may be totally foreign and uncomfortable to them. The risk of these relationships ending in divorce is very high indeed. Exceptions are the entrenched co-dependent relationships.

Co-dependent relationships, including those centered around substance or physical abuse, tend to endure because they replay the circumstances of the family of origin. Everyone knows their roles, the rules, the behaviors, and the outcome. Both survivor/partners are usually highly skilled at playing their parts and have found a way to be rewarded for doing so, no matter how strange that reward may look to others outside the relationship.

Both parties will say that they can't possibly leave for a long list of good reasons; but the real reason they stay is because they do not know any other way to be in relationship with another or with themselves and, perhaps more importantly, they have no hope that doing things differently will make things better. Their fear is that anything different can only be worse.

Only when one of the partners chooses or is forced to change in a fundamental way does the relationship either fall apart or begin to heal. Otherwise, all energy goes toward maintaining the status quo, and the same performance is repeated over and over again. In this situation, however, practice does not make perfection but leads to despair.

What one has never known, one finds very hard to envision, and what cannot be envisioned, cannot be created. If it is impossible to envision a better life, one loses hope and merely endures the days until the pain becomes overwhelming. When the pain becomes more unbearable than the fear of change and of the unknown, change at last can take place.

If, on the other hand, one holds the belief that change really is possible, then events, feelings, and behaviors are evaluated on that basis and progress can be made. A vision of change is necessary before change can take place.

Survivors rarely think to look to their own early childhoods for clues as to why their present relationships are so troubled. They focus instead on the shortcomings of their partners and the lack of mutual compatibility.

Recently I heard a story that makes this point dramatically:

A woman who grew up in an abusive family with an extremely narcissistic, controlling, and negative mother recalled a neighborhood wedding that took place when she was three years old. As a little girl, she had wanted to run across the street to be a part of the festivities, but she was not permitted to do so by her mother. Instead she watched from afar as the beautiful young bride came out of the house and walked down the street on the arm of her young husband, while friends and family smiled and offered congratulations.

As the woman first told the story, she described herself watching the radiant bride and thinking to herself, "That will never be you. You will never get married."

In fact, she has never married. As we talked about this powerful "vision" the woman had when she was three years old, I asked if she had been all alone while watching from her front yard. At first she said yes and then suddenly she remembered that she had *not* been alone that afternoon. She closed her eyes briefly trying to recall who was with her and what they were saying.

"It was my mother," the woman finally said in a very low voice. "Mother said, 'That will never be you, you will never get married.'"

The woman opened her eyes and stared at me incredulously. "So I didn't have a vision that day. My mother actually *said* what I thought just went on in my head!"

It was a powerful revelation. This woman had internalized her mother's negative programming and then blamed herself for her subsequent loneliness and sense of loss.

How she will integrate this new information, how it will change her life, no one can predict. But, at least she understands that the life she was leading was not "destiny," but intentional and malicious negative programming by a parent of a three-year-old child.

Was this also violence? I believe so, in that it violated a child's potential growth and happiness. Perhaps there is no violence greater than that.

Abusive Parenting or Caretaking

Today's children are the first generation in modern history to know that it is wrong for someone to hurt them. This awareness has been accomplished through educational institutions, media campaigns against child abuse, and increasing social consciousness. It is a fundamental shift in consciousness, one whose effects on the next generation of adults cannot be predicted.

Test cases are now being argued in court concerning the rights of minors. Children have brought these lawsuits; children now are determining where they can receive the best care and fighting to stay there. When no one rescues them from daily threats, violence, and torture in the hands of their caretakers, children are killing abusive adults.

Children are believing what they have been told and are now protecting themselves and their rights. Many adults have not yet caught on. They are mystified by this extraordinary turn of events that has happened before their very eyes, but without their full awareness or permission.

And yet, statistics show reported cases of child abuse have risen from 60,000 in 1974 to nearly three million in 1992.[7]

Until recently, it was widely believed that abusive parents were the only perpetrators of the primary long-term effects of family violence. But there are many others who caretake children, who hold power by being those upon whom children depend for their survival and well-being. These people work in adoption and foster care agencies, hospitals, doctors' offices, schools and churches, mental health institutions, and institutions for the disabled. They include lawyers, judges, elected officials, financiers, employers, and product manufacturers, all of whom hold positions of trust and responsibility that can be abused, misused, or betrayed.

What are the facts?

- Today, the federal government reports over 3 million children abused every year in America;[8]
- Another 2 million children and teenagers each year are thrown out of their homes by abusive parents or run away from incest and violence;[9]
- 600,000 babies are born each year to teenage girls;[10]
- 500,000 children are living in institutions;[11]

- 400,000 drug-addicted babies are born each year, of which approximately 50,000 are addicted to cocaine;[12]
- 3.2 million children live exclusively with their grandparents; 4% of these children are white, 12% are black. Approximately 1.6 million children live with their grandmothers only, who receive only about 50% of the financial support available to a foster parent.[13]

The Children's Defense fund offers these statistics from their 1994 report, which make "One Day in the Life of American Children":[14]

3 children die from child abuse;

9 children are murdered;

13 children die from guns;

27 children—a classroom—die from poverty;

30 children are wounded by guns;

63 babies die before they are one month old;

101 babies die before their first birthday;

145 babies are born at very low birthweight (less than 3.25 pounds);

202 children are arrested for drug offenses;

307 children are arrested for crimes of violence;

340 children are arrested for drinking or drunken driving;

480 teenagers get syphilis or gonorrhea;

636 babies are born to women who had late or no prenatal care;

801 babies are born at low birthweight (less than 5.5 pounds);

1,115 teenagers have abortions;

1,234 children run away from home;

1,340 teenagers have babies;

2,255 teenagers drop out of school;

2,350 children are in adult jails;

2,871 teenagers get pregnant;

2,860 children see their parents divorce;

2,868 babies are born into poverty;

3,325 babies are born to unmarried women;

5,314 children are arrested for some offense;

5,703 teenagers are victims of violent crime;

7,945 children are reported abused or neglected;

8,400 teenagers become sexually active;

100,000 children are homeless;

1,200,000 latchkey children come home to houses in which there is a gun;

In January 1992, *Science* magazine released a report stating that American children today are more likely than children thirty years ago to be suicidal, homicidal, and obese, to suffer from behavioral disorders, and to perform poorly on standardized achievement tests. This report was written by a Stanford University economics professor, Victor Fuchs, and research assistant, Diane Reklis. It also stated that the number of children in poverty in 1990, about 21%, is higher than in 1970 or 1980. However, between 1960 and 1970, when government spending for children's services nearly doubled, so did the number of teenage suicides, homicides, and births to teenage mothers, implying that the relation between these problems in teenagers and poverty is not as obvious as people seem to believe today.[15]

Between 1960 and 1988, government spending for American children rose only 2.9% per year, when adjusted for inflation.[16]

In 1960, 7% of American children lived in a household with no adult male present. By 1988, the number had nearly tripled to 20%. And, not surprisingly, one of every five children in the United States is poor.[17]

The so-called "underclass" of the poorly nourished and poorly educated are producing what some professionals are calling an epidemic of teen pregnancies in every region of the country. A high percentage of these babies will have dangerously low birth weights due to lack of prenatal care or are at high risk because of AIDS infection or because of drugs and alcohol consumed by the mother or father at conception or during pregnancy.

Millions of dollars are needed to keep such infants alive after birth. In some large cities, the cost of caring for these infants in public hospitals without insurance reimbursements is jeopardizing public health care availability to other citizens. If these children survive, they will most likely end up in family court, child protective service systems, foster care, orphanages, or other long-term care facilities or institutions paid for by taxpayers.

Many millions of American adults do not take adequate care of the children born to them. Either these adults do not know how to provide proper care, or they do not want children, or they vent their rage from their own childhoods on their children.

No system has yet been devised that is capable of providing healthy, long-term care for children without parents on such a massive scale. The majority of children who enter foster care as infants and toddlers do not leave foster care until they are teenagers whom no one wants, or until they reach eighteen years old and are no longer the responsibility of the system. The entire child protective services system is desperately in need of a complete overhaul, as it is no longer able to provide even basic care. In some instances, rather than providing help and protection, the system itself becomes an instrument of re-abuse and re-victimization of adult clients as well as children.

How has the quality of care for our children reached such a low?

Dr. Ray Helfer and Dr. Henry Kempe, both practicing pediatricians, alerted us to what they saw as a dangerously growing cause for concern in writing The Battered Child Syndrome in the late 1960s. In this groundbreaking book, they urged doctors and hospital emergency room attendants to be on the lookout for infants and children whose injuries could not have happened in the way or at the time reported by their parents. The publication of this book resulted in the first mandatory federal reporting laws, which were passed in 1974 and increased legislation in individual states, counties, and municipalities.

Attention was drawn first to physical abuse and life-endangering neglect, because these were the easiest forms to identify. Years later, sexual abuse of infants, children, and teenagers began to be identified. As the number of reports of abuse grew, so did public information and concern about the problem and how to handle it.

That children had rights was a topic of conversation for the first time since the introduction of child labor laws at the turn of the twentieth century. And yet, as recently as the 1970s, in most jurisdictions it was considered a crime of murder only if you killed someone else's child— not if you killed your own. Parents who murdered their own children, as long as the child was under the age of eighteen, were usually just put on probation, if, indeed, they were brought into court at all.

"Child abuse prevention and intervention are relatively new phenomena. 'Child Abuse' was not indexed in Index Medicus until 1965 and 'infanticide' was not indexed until 1970. Much of the limited medical literature on fatal child abuse has been published within the last three years. The preponderance of medical and other data are available only from uncirculated sources."[18]

The attitude of many parents toward their children is, "I brought you into this world, I gave you your life, and I can also take it away." Many adult survivors say that they heard those exact words from one or both parents repeatedly. To believe that one's child's life is one's personal property to be disposed of at will is to assume the role of god or slave master, that the parent is equal in power to the great Creator.

Often parents who hold such a belief are themselves survivors of family violence who are now behaving towards their children exactly as their parents behaved towards them years before. They have internalized the neglect, violence, and inappropriate sexual behavior they experienced as children and have identified themselves with the original aggressors, their own parents and abusers.

WORLD OF ABNORMAL REARING CYCLE

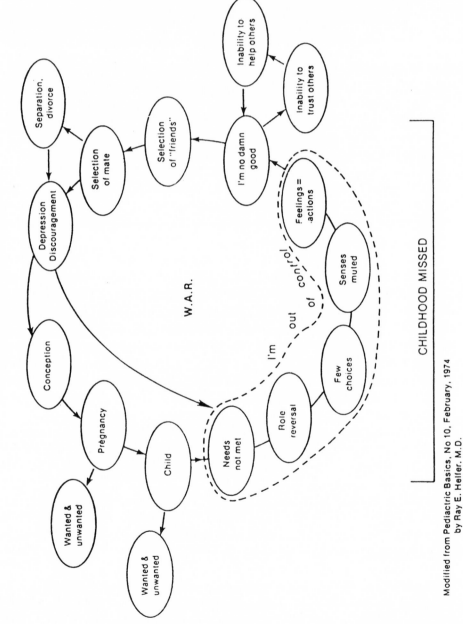

W.A.R.

CHILDHOOD MISSED

Modified from Pediatric Basics, No 10, February, 1974
by Ray E. Helfer. M.D.

Since no one ever intervened on their behalf when they were children, these adult survivors have a difficult time understanding why they should be criticized when their parents were not. If they are less violent with their children than their parents were with them, then they are even more perplexed by challenges to their parenting behavior. These survivors will tell you sincerely that they don't behave nearly as badly as their parents did toward them. Others will tell you that they were beaten half to death as children and they lived through it. They will even say that it was for their own good, that their parents loved them and did their best. Often, in the course of the same conversation, it will also become clear that today they resent all authority and have had trouble with the law.

When "love" and violent abuse are entwined in the mind of the survivor, there is a serious problem, for violence is mistaken for needed attention. In this confusion, they believe if someone loves them, they will hit, beat, humiliate, frighten, and scream at them—all for their own good. There are millions and millions of American adults who live as victims of this belief.

In this country, many children are treated by their parents and caretakers in ways that the Geneva Convention prohibits in the treatment of prisoners of war. International law prohibits starvation, the withholding of adequate shelter and food, rape, torture, or public humiliation of war prisoners; yet those punishments are common in abusive homes, where they are perpetrated on infants, toddlers, small children, and teenagers—and not just in isolated incidents, but in millions of cases every single year.

Dr. Helfer describes what he calls the World of Abnormal Child Rearing, or W.A.R.:[19] (graph on preceding page)

The conception of an unplanned or unwanted child is seen as the beginning of the cycle of abnormal childhood and that child is at high risk of abuse even before birth. Many survivors have told me that their parents admitted openly that they never wanted children and that having them ruined their [the parents'] life. Many children are made to feel guilty for a long and difficult birth. Once born, the child's needs are not met and, rather, he or she is required to serve the needs of the parent(s). The child grows up unable to make choices for his/her own well-being. The child's senses are so constantly assaulted that they close off altogether, making him/her unable to sort through, believe, or act on the barrage of information coming in from the world. Eventually strong feelings are replaced or repressed with automatic behaviors, and all that distorted learning is carried intact into adulthood.

But these behaviors, distorted as they are, enable the abused child to survive unbearable and life-threatening circumstances. As survival techniques, they will not be relinquished easily. Until new experience, new information, new skills, and new role models are sought and found, the old ways of being no matter how unsatisfactory, will be maintained. Sooner or later, however, what was perfectly reasonable behavior in the face of life-threatening events in childhood will be found totally unsuitable in adult life; but it will take a lot of faith and first-hand experience to overcome the fear of annihilation and to make the choice for change.

For the survivor, the first hurdles on the road to healing from the trauma of family violence is to have one's experience believed by at least one other person and to overcome the social denial that such things really happen. The next hurdle is to find adequate personal support (i.e., friends, spouse, therapist, self-help group, etc.) with which to work through the past pain, however long it takes, without succumbing to pressure to stop upsetting everyone else and to get the process over with quickly. The next hurdle is to align oneself with a like-minded community in order to further recovery. And the final hurdle is to live one's belief system, honoring the values one has learned to be true so that the quality of one's life begins to change to the benefit of oneself and others.

Many work places are also extremely dysfunctional and abusive. In January 1990, The New York Times reported that studies showed abuse of medical students to be a widespread phenomenon. Forty-six percent of the student body of one medical school claimed that they had been abused at some time in their training, and eighty percent of its fourth-year students reported having been abused. The studies concluded that the medical school's students were suffering "long-lasting emotional scars that may affect their care of patients as physicians" and that resulted in inferior learning and lowered self-esteem.

The Times article suggests that word of mouth regarding extremely high levels of stress, mistreatment, verbal and physical abuse, and sexual harassment has discouraged young people from enrolling in medical school and choosing medicine as a profession. These studies also indicate abuse of drugs and alcohol among students.

Judging from the high levels of abusive behavior in such institutions, chances are that their teachers and students are survivors of family abuse and violence who have never resolved issues from their own traumatic childhoods.

Upon determining that many shared this common background, some medical schools recently have made available to their students Adult Children of Alcoholics meetings, other support groups, and counselling sessions.

Dysfunctional parenting and caretaking have long been identified as the primary sources of childhood trauma. It is important to realize, however, that parents and caretakers become abusive because they themselves were abused as children. Thus survivor behaviors negatively impact both adults and children, generation after generation. However, when parents are addressed only as abusers, without acknowledgment of their own childhood histories, the resistance encountered is fierce, making constructive action all the more difficult. As a result, children are typically removed to the insufficient care of institutions, because no realistic system for family rehabilitation exists if the parents are not alcoholic, otherwise addicted, in jail, and or willing to learn alternative behaviors.

Children do not create child abuse. It is imperative to keep that truth in mind when we as a society address complex survivor issues and treatment of adult survivors. We need to create educational programs for teenagers on child care before they become parents. We need to retrain health care professionals (including physicians), judges, teachers, social workers, lawyers, police, and planners of university curricula.

In 1989, the United Nations adopted the Convention on the Rights of the Child,[20] the first comprehensive international law concerned with the treatment of children. It reads as follows:

> The Right to Survival
>   through the provision of primary health care,
>   adequate food, clean water and shelter.
> The Right to Protection
>   from abuse, neglect and exploitation, including
>   the right to special protection in times of war; and
> The Right to Develop
>   in a safe environment, through formal
>   education, constructive play, advanced health
>   care and the opportunity to participate in the
>   social, economic, religious and political life
>   of their culture, free from discrimination.

By 1992, 39 nations had ratified the United Nations Convention, providing for the rights of the child. The United States of America was not one of these nations.

Overview:
Destructive Social
Behaviors

CHAPTER 5

Overview:
Destructive Social Behaviors

This section addresses the destructive, anti-social coping behaviors directed against society by survivors as ways of coping with childhood trauma and neglect.

Anti-social means being:

1. unwilling or unable to associate with other people,

2. antagonistic or hostile toward others,

3. opposed to social order or the principles on which society is constituted.[1]

The behaviors of racism, sexism, terrorism, delinquency, crime, and homelessness all reflect one or more aspects of this definition, and each expresses a world view that has evolved directly from growing up in an atmosphere of violence, chaos, and constant misuse of power.

To develop through childhood surrounded by violence, both within and outside the home, predisposes a person to use violence in ways that probably would not occur to someone raised in a caring, supportive environment. It is this predisposition, this susceptibility created in childhood, that puts the survivor at such great risk in making and acting on life decisions. This predisposition to accept violent behavior in others and to choose to act violently oneself, as though violence were the inevitable, natural order, has been overlooked in the pursuit of finding root causes for the seemingly "senseless" violence that now confronts us everywhere.

Destructive social behavior evolves. No one is born with anti-social behaviors, they must be learned (although several anti-social behaviors may be triggered by Fetal Alcohol Syndrome, as discussed earlier.)

In early childhood, much learning of specific rudimentary skills is accomplished through imitation. A child learns language, basic interaction with others, and such skills as eating and dressing primarily by copying the parent or other caregiver. Later, children learn the larger, more complex patterns of interaction with others by example, by watching how adults behave in a given situation and using that as a guide when presented with a similar challenge. If the child receives mixed messages as to what to do, he/she will most often follow the behavior they have seen rather than the words they have heard. If a parent or caregiver is violent, the child will follow the example of violence, and the learning process thus becomes twisted into destructive rather than constructive social behavior. Many destructive social behaviors are learned before the age of ten. Eventually they will affect large numbers of innocent people, usually strangers. Their negative impact upon society is substantial and now evident in all social strata.

Many of these behaviors, once begun, are self-perpetuating, in that they tend to reinforce the destructive world view from which they were generated.

Some, such as homelessness, are very difficult to change because there is no existing social system that offers effective solutions. The circumstances behind people becoming homeless vary from post-traumatic stress after military experience and mental illness, to having suffered abuse in families of violence and survivor behaviors such as addiction and delinquency.

A person engaging in anti-social behaviors is likely to come up against some form of control, whether the military, the police, probation counsellors, social workers, or institutions such as courts, jails, prisons, shelters, mental hospitals, or secret radical membership organizations. Occasionally, anti-social behavior is actually rewarded with either a political or religious following or even an appointment to government office or the court system.

Large numbers of people who choose professions of control, such as the police or military, are survivors of physically abusive backgrounds who have identified more with the aggressor than with their own past victimization. Under such circumstances, work in these professions can also be considered survivor coping behaviors. Very often, two sets of survivors sit across the table from one another in negotiations or legal proceedings resulting from other survivor behaviors.

In violent crimes, the likelihood that the perpetrators are survivors of childhood abuse is well known and recognized; but in white collar crime—political, Wall Street, savings and loan, racist, or sexist crime—that perspective is often disregarded. And in assessing acts of war, terrorism, or national aggression, the correlation to survivor behavior is almost totally buried beneath the rhetoric of morality, religion, patriotism, and being "right."

Yet all these behaviors, and the complex decision-making process that goes into initiating them, evolve from fundamental beliefs—that force is the only real way to resolve conflict, that the world is an unsafe place, that no one can be trusted, and that the end justifies the means—that took root in the basic experience and teaching of the abusive, dysfunctional family. It is sadly the case that the dynamics of Complex Survivor Syndrome are influencing decisions and lives pervasively, on local and even international levels.

In *The Theory of Psychoanalysis*, Carl Gustav Jung writes: "The little world of childhood with its familiar surroundings is a model of the great world. The more intensively the family has stamped its character upon the child, the more it will tend to feel and see its earlier miniature world again in the bigger world of adult life. Naturally this is not a conscious, intellectual process."[2]

Perhaps it is time for us to pay serious attention to what Jung described so well and to come to understand the vast implications of his statement in relation to family violence.

As most national leaders, big city mayors, school administrators, and private citizens already know, in this decade of the nineties, there is no longer a debate between violence and non-violence as peace-making tools. That was an issue of the sixties. We are now faced with the choice between non-violence and extinction. And in order to bring violence to an end, we must come to terms with how it begins.

Racism

Racism is not just about prejudice. It is about POWER.

Racism is not just about skin color, it is about FEAR.

The desire to have power over others and the fear of domination by others are two primary survivor traits.

The desire for extraordinary power over others in adulthood most likely takes seed when a child experiences powerlessness in the hands of an adult upon whom he or she depends and who wields power in ways that are violent or sadistic. Under such circumstances, fear is a reasonable response to be expected. What people do with that fear as they mature into adolescence and adulthood, however, will lead either to new problems or creative solutions for living a healthy life.

It is interesting to note, in modern history, how may countries associated with very aggressive nationalistic behavior have espoused a racist philosophy. Germany under the Nazis was anti-Semitic and fatally paranoid about Aryan supremacy and racial purity. The Japanese and other oriental cultures hold fierce, rigid beliefs regarding the maintenance of "pure blood" and reject from top echelons of society any citizens of mixed blood. Children of GI's left behind with their Asian mothers after WWII and the wars in Korea and Viet Nam belong neither to occident nor orient and have been denied schooling, health care, and decent jobs.

The former Soviet Union's fifteen republics were ethnically diverse, but all were subjected to Russiafication, the subjugation of all races other than Russian, by the Soviet central government. Today ethnic clashes abound in nearly every region.

In Mexico and Central and South America, the native peoples have been practically enslaved by the European conquerors who are now running these, countries. Uprisings occur regularly.

In the United States, the Native American nations have nearly been destroyed, and their surviving peoples are not treated as full citizens. Legal enslavement of blacks was abolished only one hundred and forty years ago, and many new immigrants are still subject to virtual, although illegal, bondage.

In Europe, Great Britain, and Arab countries, racial tension erupts over the numbers of third world workers, all people of color, who sign on to do work no one else will do in order to send money home to their underdeveloped countries.

Until the Gulf War, Israel had the same situation with the Palestinians, but now Soviet immigrants are taking their jobs while they are under curfew.

Racism, the belief that one race is inherently superior to and entitled to dominate over another, has been used to justify scapegoating and the abuse of power. It is an attempt by one person or group of people to feel "better than" or "more than" another person or group of people with no qualitative basis other than that of cultural background.

Sometimes racism is the result of growing up in a racist household.

Sometimes racism is the result of social pressure, regional cultural practices, and/or even a national policy (e.g., South Africa).

Negative personal experiences associated with racial differences (e.g., mandatory school busing) that evoke feelings of powerlessness or fear can sometimes lead to racist attitudes; but other factors in a person's adult life and childhood history will influence whether the negative experience is transmuted constructively or used to fuel intolerance.

Children never permitted to think or feel differently from the adults upon whom they depend and who consequently have power over them will themselves grow up to be rigid, intolerant, narrow-minded adults.

Leaders of totalitarian regimes permit only one way of thinking—theirs. Heads of totalitarian families behave the same way, even in a democracy. Children raised in such families are prone to either regarding anyone in power, particularly males, as absolute authorities, or, at the opposite extreme, rebelling against all authority. They may also take out anger on those they judge to be "less than" themselves as a way of gaining a feeling of power and reducing feelings of fear fed by a sense of their own inadequacy.

As a nation we have become increasingly violent in our intolerance of the differences of others. In his book, *Blood and Belonging: Journeys into the New Nationalism*, Michael Ignatieff writes, "The more strongly you feel the bonds of belonging to your own group, the more hostile, the more violent will your feelings be toward outsiders. When nationalists claim that national belonging is the overridingly important form of all belonging, they mean that there is no other form of belonging—to your family, work, or friends—that is secure if you do not have a nation to protect you."[3] Although Mr. Ignatieff is writing about international nationalism, this could as easily be said about American gangs or hate groups that replace families, particularly neglectful, absent, or violent families.

We permit more and more censorship. We seem to need to scapegoat people or groups in order to justify and promote our aggressive policies.

These two dynamics of scapegoating and identification with the aggressor are first learned in the dysfunctional family.

The virulence of racism in this country is clear in the following statistics:

- In 1991, 346 white supremacy groups were operating in the United States, up 27% from 1990 and a record high.[4]

- Black and Hispanic Americans faced discrimination more than 50% of the time in attempting to rent or buy homes in 25 metropolitan areas.[5]

- Blacks have fewer assets than whites: less savings, fewer checking accounts, less equity in home or business.[6] Only 7% have stocks or mutual funds or IRA/Keoghs for retirement.[7]

- The average net worth of black households is only 23% of white households.[8]

- Nearly one million illegal immigrants were arrested in 1991-92, almost all of whom were Hispanic.[9]

- The Commission on the African-American Male[10] reports:

  *40% of young black men do not graduate from high school;

  *40% of all black male adults are functionally illiterate;

  *More young black men are under control of the criminal justice system than are enrolled in college;

  *Life expectancy for black males is 65.2 years;

  *The homicide rate for black men between 20 to 29 years old is six times higher than for the rest of the population of the same age and homicide is the leading cause of death for black males 15 to 24 years old;

  *Suicide is the third leading cause of death among young black males;

- The Southern Poverty Law Center reported in 1991:

  *A record high 346 white supremacy groups are operating in the U.S.A., up 27% from 1990;

  *Hate crimes doubled between 1990 to 1991, totalling 101 for the nation for both years. This was the fourth year of increase. The crimes ranged from murder (25) to cross-burnings, assault, bombings, and arson;

  *In 1992, two men running for President of the United States put forth racially biased statements and political positions.

Because of the violence against them from outside and inside their communities, national attention has been focused primarily on black men as victims of racism; but there is another kind of violence, also the result of racism, that has affected black women.

It is the black women who are left to grieve for their lost brothers, lovers, husband, father, and sons, and to raise single-handedly their orphaned or abandoned children. Black women have to make their way in a job market that is unfriendly to all women, and particularly so to black women wanting more than menial or service employment.

These are the facts of life that black women face in America in the 1990s.[11]

- Single mothers are raising 54% of America's black children;
- 44% of all black children live in poverty;
- For all black families with children under 18 years old and both parents present, the median annual income is $35,720;
- For black families headed by a woman and with children under 18, the annual income is $10,310;
- 56% of black children in households headed by a woman live below the official government poverty line;
- 52% of American women with AIDS are black (black men are only 25% of the U.S. male AIDS population);
- 52% of all HIV babies are black, most born and raised by single mothers.

The black woman must confront sexual discrimination as well as racial bias, so that she has two battles to fight, on her own. If she accepts the general belief that her brothers have the more difficult time of it and that race is a more important issue than sex, then the considerable problems she faces as a woman are denied their equal seriousness and importance. This dismissal of the black woman's problems and challenges is a disrespect for the woman herself that evokes anger, resentment, guilt, and shame.

It is no surprise that many black women are physically abusive toward their children. In an attempt to "keep the kids in line," they use the only means they know: violence. And violence produces more violence, as we see day after day.

> Where justice is denied, where poverty is enforced, where ignorance prevails, and where any one class is made to feel that society is in an organized conspiracy to oppress, rob, and degrade them, neither persons nor property will be safe.
>
> *Frederick Douglass* (April 1886)
>
> Speech on the twenty-fourth anniversary of Emancipation in the District of Columbia, Washington, D.C.

Sexism

Sexual prejudice tends to fall into one of two major categories: prejudice against gender and prejudice against sexual orientation. Prejudice is learned behavior. Prejudice is a form of social violence toward the rights of others. For survivors of family violence, who grew up with so little self-esteem, prejudice is way of feeling superior to others.

The term sexism today is most often applied to prejudicial treatment of women; however, it also takes the form of prejudice against men and against homosexuals.

First, in terms of prejudice against gender, and specifically against women, what are the facts?

- Every 15 seconds, a woman will be battered by her spouse, boyfriend, or male sexual partner. These crimes, often called domestic or family violence, are the leading cause of injury to women between the ages of 15 and 45;

- Between 2 and 4 million women will be severely assaulted by their male partners each year, and at least 2,000 of those women will die as a result;

- Domestic violence (household terrorism) is the leading cause of injury to women in the United States;

- Most women cannot get legal protection against those who have hurt them and, as a result, the majority of male batterers are neither in jail nor required to seek treatment.

The United States Department of Education study of the high school class of 1972,[12] tracking the relative progress of male and female students from graduation through age 32, found that:

- Women outperformed men at every level of education and in every subject, including college level math, but their place in the labor market in no way rewards this superior performance;

- Between the ages of 25 and 32, a much higher percentage of women than men were unemployed, no matter what educational degree they had earned;

- In 26 to 33 occupations, men were paid more than women without children;
- On the job, women developed better work relationships and better skills;
- In 1990, women held less than 3% of top jobs at Fortune 500 companies. Of the 6,502 executives at the level of vice president and above, only 175 were women.

During the Hill-Thomas hearings, when the nation watched a Senate committee of white middle-aged men—and not one woman—in judgment of a female black law professor, without even a thorough hearing of the charges she was making, the effect was catalytic. The public response to the Hill-Thomas confrontation made it undeniably clear that sexual harassment of women in the work place is a common occurrence.

Sexual harassment can range from insistent flirting to sexual slavery. At the latter extreme, victims have been kidnapped and forced into sexual behaviors against their will. Often in such cases, the victims are then murdered; but once in a while they escape their captors to tell their grisly story.

Between these extremes, there is sexist behavior toward women in the workplace that creates an atmosphere of daily discomfort, with sexual references, inappropriate and unwelcome touching, sexualized teasing, and off-color jokes. The woman comes to dread each such encounter and fears losing opportunities for promotion if she refuses to participate or to be coerced.

Sexual harassment may be as much an issue of abuse of power as of sexism. The assertion of power or dominance over another in any form has an aspect of inner violence to it; in this case, the victim may lose her/his job, promotion, reputation, and/or self-respect in the process of either trying to fend off or accommodate the aggressor. Although men have reported being sexually harassed as well, the victims in most cases are women.

The American Management Association researched 500 companies in preparing a report on how sexual harassment claims had been resolved in the five years just previous to 1991.[13]

- 36% of all cases surveyed were resolved through counselling or mediation;
- 27% of these cases resulted in a formal reprimand;
- In 17% of cases surveyed, the complaint was dismissed without action;
- Probation or suspension of the accused offender occurred in 14% of cases;

• In 6% of cases the offender resigned.

At the time of Anita Hill's employment with Clarence Thomas, none of these options was available, nor were laws yet in place for victims of sexual harassment.

———•◦•———

Our national health care system places the act of childbirth in the cold and alienating environment of hospital operating rooms, discourages breastfeeding, and prevents the licensing of nurse midwifes, thus increasing both trauma and expense in the birth process. In addition, some religions and political factions, in trying to outlaw abortion, are once again threatening to violate every woman's right to determine what happens to her own body. While the United States Constitution guarantees separation of church and state, this battle over women's rights is primarily between religious and secular points of view.

Strides have been made toward paying men and women equally for equal work, but as a nation we have no commitment to day care as a vital component of the workplace environment, nor to prenatal care and early childhood education, all practices long established in Europe, Canada, Japan, the former Soviet Union, and China. And women represent over 50% of the population and work force in this country.

There are no counterparts to these issues in the experience of men.

———•◦•———

Because of homophobia or sexist behavior against lesbians and homosexual men, this sector of the population has tended to gather in larger cities where their numbers can influence decisions affecting their environment. Gangs roam streets in the gay sections of cities, looking to assault gay men.

Some communities have considered legislation against lesbian women and gay men, causing these men and women to feel unsafe in their own neighborhoods. Such legislation was successfully passed in Denver, Colorado, but defeated elsewhere.

Sexist behavior, in whatever form, is violating behavior in that it disrespects and acts against the inherent nature of another human being. Sexism judges a person to be fundamentally flawed by virtue of the sexual nature they were born to, a condition over which they had no control whatsoever.

One cannot have self-esteem without a self. If one's gender, a fundamental aspect of selfhood and identity, is treated with scorn, shame, and neglect, then one easily becomes unacceptable to oneself as well as to others. This rejection of the self creates rage that may be expressed as depression, surface anger, and self-abuse.

There are women who spend most of their lives trying to be "sons" for their fathers. There are men who devote their lives to their mothers, trying to make up for their not having been born as daughters. Many survivors, knowing that their gender was a great disappointment to their parents, struggle throughout their lives to validate themselves, whether by becoming a "super"-male or "super"-female or by choosing to identify more with the opposite sex.

In a society where sexist behavior is endorsed by religions or culturally reinforced, the survivor, who is always vulnerable to re-abuse, is especially at risk.

A person need not be a feminist or active in the men's movement to behave in a non-sexist way. All they need do is to recognize each person as a unique individual rather than the representative of some general quality to be judged or punished.

Terrorism

Terrorism is usually thought of in an international context as random guerrilla attacks on civilians and businesses by political or religious fanatics wanting to win control by fear as much as by force, with maximum effect and minimum cost to the perpetrators. But terrorism is also perpetrated within families and local communities, at home, and on the streets.

"Domestic violence" is terrorism, household terrorism. It operates in the secrecy of the home, at random and without warning, against innocent, defenseless people, primarily women and children of both sexes. This form of terrorism also controls by fear. Its effects on survivors are severe and long-term.

Terrorism is learned behavior. It is learned first in the home, from parents, those very people upon whom a child depends for love and protection. It is not hard to terrorize a small, helpless child when the person doing the terrorizing is a full-grown adult. The advantage of physical size alone is enough if it is used against the child rather than for his or her protection. A blow to the face or head with an open hand or closed fist can easily knock a child unconscious or cause serious brain damage. Throwing or shaking a child can cause death or severe learning disabilities. Burning, cutting, or beating a child can leave emotional as well as physical scars. Yelling, cursing, or humiliating a child can leave him or her feeling valueless, damned, disgusting, and shameful.

Children can do nothing against such attacks. They cannot defend themselves, they cannot prevent the attacks or stop them once they have begun, and usually they cannot run away from them either.

But the child's psyche works overtime to try to keep him or her alive. If staying alive means numbing the body, mind, and/or spirit, then that is what the child will do. The body is numbed against physical pain and the mind is numbed against psychic and emotional pain and frequently against feelings of love, compassion for others, guilt, and remorse as well. Those feelings and responses are literally beaten out of the child by his or her parents. The child quickly learns that numbing makes everyday life easier to bare. With sustained abuse, more and more facets and responses of the self are relegated to numbness, and it takes greater and greater stimulation to evoke any response whatsoever. The child may become a "bystander" to his own pain, observing it as if it were happening to somebody else.

It is a terrible irony of living with violence that the abused child must choose a behavior as close to being dead as possible in order to remain alive.

Not long ago, the Fox Television network sponsored a night of "truce" to bring Los Angeles youth gangs together. A young African-American comic performed a routine about his relationship with his grandmother and how she had raised him. The comic described how his grandmother once "slapped him into retarded." He assumed the twisted stance of a disabled person, and his audience laughed like crazy, nodding their heads in recognition.

Violent behavior towards little children does *not* teach good behavior; it teaches violence, and only violence. The only variable is whether the child turns that violence against himself through drug use and other self-destructive acts or against the environment and others on the streets, in relationships, politics, repressive social policies, or wars.

In 1991, *The Washington Post* ran a series of interviews with young men in jail on charges of drug trafficking, assault with a deadly weapon, and/or murder. Many said that they carried guns not just for safety, but power, and that the kind of gun one carried determined one's status: from revolver, to semi-automatic, to assault weapon at the top. They said there was "no problem" in acquiring as many guns as one wanted. They described themselves as becoming addicted to the weapons and their use, even likening gun use to sex. They said that shooting people was "fun."

None of these men seemed to feel any remorse; they were more likely to think of themselves as resembling movie heroes, like those played by Charles Bronson, John Wayne, Clint Eastwood, and others, who are rewarded for blowing people away.

Interestingly enough, the older inmates, even those convicted of murder, viewed these new recruits as being much tougher and meaner than themselves. One inmate in his forties described his generation as the hustlers, while these young men were "rustlers," who would do in even their grandmothers.

Our national policy *protects* the proliferation of guns. President Bush refused to ban the over-the-counter sale of assault weapons. Assault weapons are not designed for hunting deer; they are used to gun down children on school grounds and to massacre patrons in coffee shops. They have killed homeowners, storekeepers, and babies in their cribs when bullets from "drive-by" shootings have gone astray.

Every day more innocent people are killed. The responsibility for these deaths belongs with the politician who bowed to the gun lobby as well as the man who shot the bullets.

Public policy in the United States pays lip service to the safety, protection, and health of children and to the war on crime and drugs but continues to protect and defend the manufacturers of violence, whether they are the makers of guns and drugs or the uneducated, sadistic parents of children. Meanwhile, television advertising and the entertainment industry glorify deviant, violent behavior, turning sociopaths into heroes to be worshipped and emulated by disaffected and already angry street kids.

Some areas of our big cities can only be described as war zones. The killing continues unabated, spilling over into schools, buses, parks, commuter trains, and restaurants. Many big city schools have had to use money budgeted for teachers, instructional materials, and after-school programs to install the same metal detectors used in airports as protection against international terrorists to protect children against the terrorist attacks of other children. These conditions are quickly spreading out from big cities to small towns and suburbs as well.

Worst of all, as a society we have become so numb to violence that this horrifying situation is almost taken for granted. There seems to be a "hands-off" policy in our country toward the loss and destruction on an entire generation of young people.

Even if nothing else is done to make the crisis worse, this attitude of avoidance and denial permits the violence to continue. It permits the continuation of disastrous child-care and parenting practices, of the under-education of our young, and of the rule of domination.

The message of international terrorism carried to its extreme is, "If I cannot live the way I want, neither will you live as you want." This attitude was horribly exemplified during the Gulf War of 1991, when retreating Iraqi troops set fire to hundreds of oil wells. The smoke from the burning wells blocked the sun, creating a condition of "nuclear winter" that is already resulting in large-scale ecological ruination and crop failures. The health of millions of completely innocent people all over the Mideast and in China and Russia has been endangered.

Saddam Hussein, who instigated the Gulf War by ordering his troops to invade a neighboring country, certainly qualifies as a terrorist both domestically and internationally. He has reportedly killed his own advisors for bringing him "bad" news. He has used chemical weapons to kill Kurdish people, Iraq's racial minority population; he may also have used chemical warfare against the coalition/American troops (although the U.S. military is as slow to substantiate that health risk as they were with agent orange after-effects following Viet Nam); he allowed his troops to loot, rape, and torture civilians; and he called publicly for terrorist attacks on the people of the U.S. and coalition countries—all in the name of an Islamic holy war against the western infidels.

From what little has been written about Saddam Hussein's early life, it appears that he was orphaned or his father died when he was less than a year old. He was then raised by his uncle, a radical military man, until school age. Later, Saddam was brutally and sadistically mistreated and beaten by his stepfather until he joined the military at fourteen years old.

People like Saddam Hussein do not appear out of thin air as pathological adults. Even Saddam Hussein began as an innocent child who, through years of abandonment and abuse, developed skills that enabled him to survive. In the language of psychology, he identified with the aggressor and developed an extreme personality disorder called "malignant narcissism," by which he was driven to prove himself bigger and better and more powerful than he felt as a child.

Adolf Hitler was systematically, viciously, and brutally terrified, beaten, and humiliated by caretaker adults over many years. He, like Hussein, was charismatic to his people, but flew into narcissistic rages, and maintained power by spreading fear and terrorism.

Terrorism creates an atmosphere of apprehension. Over time, apprehension becomes a state of constant anxiety, fearfulness, hyper-vigilance, and rage. In such a state, there is no sense of safety. Any place can be dangerous, anyone can be an enemy.

Alice Miller, in her book *For Your Own Good*, brilliantly suggests that the atmosphere created by a terrorist regime is exactly the same as that found in an abusive home. The essential qualities are identical. In both situations, fear supplants all softer human qualities over long periods of time, creating only anger and the need for retaliation.

These conditions created by terrorism are those prevailing in the streets of American cities, in Lebanon, Sarajevo, Northern Ireland, South Africa, the Philippines, the Middle East, and much of Central America. To make matters worse, industrialized nations, including the United States, are selling terrorist organizations the supplies with which to carry out their threats.

Abusive families, intolerant parents, create children ready to wage wars. It's easy for abused children to take what they've learned from their families onto the streets and vent it on others. It's even easier to take it into the military where such behavior can be directed against a national enemy and rewarded as patriotism.

This is how the powerless can turn the tables and become the powerful, how a fearful child can become the most feared of men, how the downtrodden and outcast find a place of belonging and are glamorized by the media into a sort of terrorist stardom.

Michael Ignatieff, in his book *Blood and Belonging: Journeys into the New Nationalism*, writes "most nationalist violence is perpetuated by a small minority of males between the ages of eighteen and twenty-five. Until I had encountered...young males intoxicated by the power of guns on their hip, I had not understood how deeply pleasurable it is, for some, to have the power of life and death in their hands...men who love the ruins, loved the destruction." He goes on to say that he believes this new nationalism is actually a rebellion of young men against the father state, that rule of law, order, logic, and self-defense against which the sons are raging with the "staggering gratuitousness and bestiality of nationalist violence." He surmises that psychologically "nationalism exists to warrant and legitimize the son's vengeance against the father."[14]

In millions of homes in the United States, dysfunctional parents and violent families are creating exactly the conditions necessary to produce a new generation of terrorists, whether domestic or international. The data substantiating this trend is available and public, and still Americans cling to the belief that terrorist activity exists only in the Middle East, Northern Ireland, and other faraway places.

Perhaps it is as yet too difficult to look at ourselves with the same scrutiny we apply to our enemies. And yet, as the cartoon character Pogo once said, "We have met the enemy and he is us."

Juvenile Delinquency

If there is no hope that tomorrow will be any different from today, and if today is intolerable, there is nothing to stop you from taking what you want and doing as you please. In children, adolescents, and the underclass, that behavior is called *delinquency*. In adults in the top echelons of society and business, that behavior is called being successful. Their motivations may differ, but both the "delinquents" and the "successful" adults are intent on taking what they want and doing as they please without regard for the rights of others. And the "successful" adults are rewarded for it, while the "delinquents" are punished.

Delinquent behavior, whether in children, adolescents, or adults, is childish and anti-social behavior and usually not in the long-term best interests of its perpetrators.

Most adolescent delinquents are extremely dependent upon their peer groups, primarily because they have no functioning families, effective parenting, nurturing, or positive adult role models to rely on. These young people come from all ethnic backgrounds and live in middle- and upper-class neighborhoods as well as in ghettos. We hear most about black and hispanic gangs running drugs, stealing, and mugging; but there are also white gangs, such as neo-nazis and skin-heads, that for adults may take on the functions of survivalist or para-military groups, political parties or lobbying organizations, while still maintaining their essential character and intent.

Membership in a gang provides a sense of power or belonging. It takes the place of kinship. The gang is the post-modern "family," complete with codes of protection and loyalty for its members. That they are substitutes for families is what gives the groups their psychological power and makes it so difficult for them to break up or dissolve.

The shared desire for money, power, and violence joins people together both at the top and at the bottom of our social structure. At the top are the "good old boy" network and the military-industrial complex that General Eisenhower cautioned us against a generation ago, of which the powerful gun lobby and the defense contractors are striking examples.

At the other end of the social spectrum, there are the gangs in our inner cities, whose territories have come to resemble war zones. Fire, police, and ambulance services often will not venture into such areas on weekends or at the height of violent sprees, from fear for their lives. A kind of barbarism now prevails in many cities that nobody wants to talk about.

Police alone cannot solve these problems because crime is not their real cause and because police under increasing stress or frustration may contribute to crime with racism and excessive violence.

The real cause of inner city turmoil is the violent, abusive family, or, more accurately, the disintegration of the family as a positive social unit. This root cause is reflected in other factors contributing to the decline of our cities, including the lack of adequate prenatal care, education, jobs, affordable housing, and self-esteem, and the predominance of drugs, drugs, and more drugs. Drugs are both the fuel and the fire.

Most delinquents who show up in juvenile courts had initial contact with the system years earlier, as innocent victims in divorce, custody, or support payment hearings, or as abused children appearing before dependency courts for protection and intervention, which they probably never received.

Many of these young people have been in and out of the social services system since birth. They have been abused, abandoned, and neglected, placed in dozens of foster and group homes, eventually to find themselves in juvenile court and detention camps.

Very little is yet known about biological causes of delinquent behavior, such as fetal alcohol syndrome (FAS). How many young people currently in detention camps, being processed through juvenile courts, or serving time for crimes of violence are actually suffering the results of fetal alcohol syndrome? No one knows. But FAS may be one explanation for the high incidence of seemingly "senseless" delinquent behavior in affluent neighborhoods; for a pregnant woman in a wealthy suburb can be just as addicted to alcohol as her sister in the slums or working in an office.

Truancy (staying out of school without permission) is another form of delinquent behavior in children and adolescents with many different causes: boredom, inability to read, learning/attention span problems, brain damage as a result of the mother's use of drugs or alcohol during pregnancy, and a lack of legitimate job prospects. Many truants' parents never finished school and may not be much more than children themselves.

High school counselors know that many, many communities simply have nothing better to offer the young person than the money and prestige of selling drugs. The job market offers limited, usually only minimum-wage, possibilities to high school students or graduates, and everyone knows you can't live on the minimum wage. There is little incentive for young people to give up their gangs and lucrative drug dealing.

Drugs and/or alcohol use is also another form of delinquency, in this case turned against oneself rather than others.

Generalized rebellious behavior has always been associated with adolescence, the time when young people define themselves as separate from their parents and learn to make choices in the world. When the onset of adolescence is coupled with a childhood of abuse in an aggressively authoritarian house, delinquent behavior (getting into fights, getting drunk, bullying others, getting into trouble at school) is likely and understandable.

For many years, some states had laws concerning "recalcitrant" children, children who resisted authority or were otherwise difficult. Until the latter part of this century, a parent could take whatever measures he or she deemed necessary with such a child, including taking the child's life.

Even after slavery in the United States was abolished, women and children of both sexes were still legally in bondage to the male head of the household. Adult females and children had no civil rights but were considered the "chattel," or personal property of the male. There are some still alive today who were also alive when the law described women and children as a separate class with few or no rights of their own.

When I was growing up, a parent could have police remove the child from the home simply by labeling him/her "incorrigible." It was the word of the parent against the word of the child, without an impartial hearing or influence. When parents no longer wanted to cope with their children, this was a quick solution.

Today, it's the insurance companies and medical community that are assisting upper-income parents in removing children from the home. An *Utne Reader* survey article on youth reveals that since 1980, adolescent psychiatric admissions have risen between 250% and 400%. The Children's Defense Fund claims that 40% of the adolescent psychiatric admissions are inappropriate; other sources estimate the number to be as high as 75%. The number of hospitals treating adolescents psychiatrically had risen from 220 in 1984 to 341 in 1988. Why? Because insurance companies pay 80 to 100% for inpatient care and the hospitals make between $500 to $1,000 per day during the first 30 to 75 days. Hospitalizing "difficult" children has become a relatively easy—and inexpensive, at least for the parents—recourse for getting them out of the way.[15]

Of course, the young person's admission to the hospital is usually not voluntary, and he or she cannot get out without permission from someone else—conditions which could be considered in violation of civil rights.

The diagnoses under which many of these middle- and upper-class children are hospitalized include "conduct disorder" and "oppositional deficit disorder," which others simply call classic teenage behavior. Many girls—but not boys—are hospitalized for sexual promiscuity, a behavior often found in children who have been inappropriately sexualized at a young age or who are hungry for the affection and recognition their parents deny them.

Parents who institutionalize their children whenever their behavior needs attention, and the insurance companies that support them in doing so, are perpetuating a subtle form of violence over the civil rights of children instead of providing healthy parenting and nurturing. The implication of this form of violence is that people are disposable unless they behave in a way that is convenient and comfortable to those in authority.

Running away from home is sometimes considered delinquent behavior in children, but "throwing away" children (not permitting them to live at home while they're still underage) is not considered delinquent behavior in parent adults. No reparation to the children is required from the parents and no shelter is provided for them by authorities *unless* they resort to committing crimes in order to support themselves.

Children who are runaways almost always have been physically or sexually abused over time. Most runaways and throwaways end up in large cities. Many use drugs and/or alcohol. Many contact AIDS. Most will not live past the age of thirty-five, which is about the same life expectancy of people in the Middle Ages, nearly one thousand years ago.

Today, many teenagers escaping homes of abuse and violence are recruited to work in pornography and prostitution. Add to them the "throwaways," and a large group of young people is formed, many of whom are under sixteen and so too young to obtain a legal work permit. Without a work permit, they can't get legitimate work, even at minimum wage. Or if they can get a permit, teenagers are often paid less than minimum wage in the belief that they have families who support them.

Although statistics are suspiciously few and difficult to obtain, there are an estimated two million teenage runaways and throwaways.

When I was Commissioner for Children's Services in Los Angeles in the 1980s, our county of eight million had only eighteen bed spaces for nondelinquent teenagers whose families refused to provide for them.

Americans almost worship the idea of youth, but as a society we give little real thought or concern to our young people. A shocking number of adults actively dislike or claim to hate their children and cannot wait to get rid of them. We are quick to blame these children for their misdeeds, yet very slow to consider the true causes of their delinquency.

Meanwhile, delinquent behavior is carried into adulthood to take such forms as carrying a gun without a permit, accumulating and not paying parking tickets, and shirking financial and other obligations so that one is always "looking over one's shoulder" and feeling oneself "just one step ahead of the law."

Recently, some 355 of a total 432 members of the House of Representatives were discovered to have written many thousands of checks without sufficient funds. This is a perfect example of adult delinquent behavior on a massive scale. The privileges of high public office were arrogantly abused, resulting in financial delinquency and the violation of public trust.

When the Congressmen were threatened with exposure by the media for the bounced checks, the government attempted to protect them and "keep the secret" about the extent of the misconduct. This situation closely parallels that in an abusive family when the authorities (parents) attempt to deny or cover up their own dysfunctional and/or abusive behaviors at the expense of their children (the public).

Each kind of delinquent behavior has its own place in Complex Survivor Syndrome and as a separate spoke on the Survivor's Wheel, as well as within other survivor behaviors.

Crime

"Violence begets violence," observed Martin Luther King.

There are many kinds of violent crime. Criminal behavior is defined as that which breaks a law or laws. Generally speaking, laws exist to protect people, possessions, and institutions from theft or violation by others. Criminal behavior takes something without obtaining permission, without adequate compensation for its value, usually by force or subterfuge, and always, when it is violent, by inflicting physical or mental harm on the victim.

During periods of social transformation, when collective value systems change relatively rapidly, some behaviors are newly recognized as criminal, while no laws yet exist to prohibit them At the same time, some laws already in existence do not work as they were envisioned and need to be changed or eliminated. Prohibition is an example of one of those laws. While these changes are occurring, some chaos can be expected. I believe we are in such a period of change today.

The murder rate grew 25% in the United States between 1985 and 1991. In 1990, nearly 24,000 people were killed, about 1,000 of them children.[16]

But we don't need statistics to tell us we have a high crime rate in this country. We live with the constant reminders of alarm systems, bars on our windows and doors, guards in our elementary schools, and fear in our hearts as we go out at night or walk down an empty street.

Who among us doesn't know at least one victim of a mugging, car theft, rape, or fraud? How many of us have not been conned at least once by business partners, investment schemes, real estate deals, or a spouse? How many have not lost money to unscrupulous repair or construction contractors, junk bond brokers, real estate syndications, lawyers, savings and loan or insurance companies?

The streets are not safe. Our homes are not safe. Our banks are not safe. Our schools are not safe. Work places are not safe. Travel is not safe.

If they survive the callous health care system, our elderly are sitting ducks for con artists, thieves, and murderers. Our children are targets for dope dealers and sexual exploitation. Our workers are subjected to serious hazards as a result of employer irresponsibility regarding the health and safety of employees. We all are prey to "get rich quick" scams and a lottery that promises to provide for community service improvement but does not.

Movies and television programs glorify macho violence and horror. Network television exists primarily to sell commercials and a materialistic value system. Over all, the media are promoting a kind of dehumanization by which human beings are manipulated and treated with the same sensitivity as pieces of furniture, while encouraging adolescent attitudes and the desire for instant solutions to complex problems. It is difficult to measure the influence of these attitudes on the public, but surely it is not negligible.

Neither con artists nor those who commit crimes of violence see their victims as people, as fellow human beings. In order to do what they do, they have cut off all feelings but those of the thrill of the game and of empowerment at getting the job done.

Every day the news carries stories from Wall Street, Main Street, and Skid Row about people to whom lying, falsifying accounts, and breaking contracts have become standard business practices. In such behaviors, there is no awareness of right and wrong, good and bad, no feeling for the pain caused to others. Such behaviors were once called amoral; today they are called sociopathic.

In 1974, a study was undertaken at San Quentin prison, California, that revealed that 100% of the inmates convicted of and serving time for crimes of violence against others were severely abused as children.

In 1992, the National Institute of Justice released a long-term study on the effects of childhood trauma and family violence. The study followed 1,575 cases from childhood through young adulthood and reported that "being abused or neglected as a child increased the likelihood of arrest as a juvenile by fifty-three percent, as an adult by thirty-eight percent, and for violent crime by thirty-eight percent."[17]

These findings have not been used in determining corrective action. Meanwhile, more and more prisons are being built and filled. Prisons have turned into breeding grounds for social dysfunction, drugs, abuse, rape, institutional tyranny, and gang violence.

The prison population is now about one million. It costs taxpayers over $20,000 a year to house and feed one prisoner.[18] As a result of overcrowding and these high costs, most prisoners, including murderers, will serve only a part of their sentences before being paroled and returned to society.

Ann Rule, a crime writer and former policewoman, told me that in her years of working with and writing about serial killers, she discovered that no matter how different their victim types or methods of murder, they all had one thing in common: *every one of them had been severely physically abused as a child*. Many also had been sexually abused and some had been systematically tortured by their parents.

Law enforcement institutions still refuse to understand the terrible and long-term nature of the impact of physical and/or sexual abuse upon the life of a child. As in the case of a serial killer, we see the appalling results only through the tragedies of their victims. The murderer's early life is not investigated, and while he is charged as a perpetrator of crime, those who victimized him get off scott free and are rarely even questioned.

In an April 1992 magazine interview, Robert Ressler, cofounder of the FBI's psychological profiling program and now a private consultant on criminal behaviors, stated that many serial killers displayed delinquent behaviors, such as interest in pornography, sadistic behavior toward other children or animals, and setting fires, in early childhood, and confirmed other findings that many had been physically or emotionally abused. Mr. Ressler made a chilling prediction: "America is going to turn into *A Clockwork Orange* [a film made by Stanley Kubrick in the 1960s about a group of sociopathic/psychopathic youth who terrorized a city]. The sexual psychopath will become the norm . . . We're raising new monsters for new generations. Once they've stepped over the threshold, they're gone. There is no treatment." However, Mr. Ressler then dismisses as irrelevant the factors that are behind the creation of these "new monsters." The "why" never caught anybody, he says!

But it is only in addressing directly the effects of childhood abuse, neglect, exploitation, and humiliation that we have any hope of understanding what produces the serial killer, the mass murderer, the con man, and so many other malfunctioning people and institutions in our society today.

Some years ago, I received a long letter from a man serving time in prison for incest. He wrote that he had not realized that there was anything wrong with his behavior until he saw a TV movie about incest. After much agonizing and soul searching, he turned himself in to authorities. His family was outraged that he did so, which is not surprising since, according to my correspondent, thirty-seven of its members were engaged in sexual abuse and incest. Male and female adults were having sexual relationships with both male and female children, step-children, nieces, nephews, etc. No other person in his family had ever been caught, reported, or felt any sense of guilt about his or her behavior.

In this family, as in many others, these violations are so common and socially accepted by those in the immediate environment that they are seen as normative behavior.

On a different level, the "merger mania" of the 1980s was another socially accepted criminal behavior. "Merger mania" took root in our culture's greed and grew with the invention of junk bonds. Many of these bonds did indeed turn out to be worthless junk, and the voluminous trading of them created serious problems for savings and loan and life insurance companies; but "merger mania" went unapprehended until after it had struck lethal blows to many American businesses, caused the national debt to skyrocket, and forced the taxpayer to foot the bill.

In this disgraceful debacle, we were treated to reports of Wall Street brokers being handcuffed and arrested en masse, cabinet members and presidential advisors being accused of misconduct and conflict of interest while in office, and senators and even a president's son being accused of aiding and abetting the savings and loan disaster.

Sad to say, most crimes today go unpunished. Our system of justice has fallen apart, and our criminals know it. Individuals and businesses no longer feel obliged to keep contractual promises, because they know that most people either can't afford legal costs or don't want to tie up the years it takes for a case to come up in civil court. Drug dealers hire minors under sixteen years old to commit felonies because most jurisdictions do not prosecute children under the same laws as adults. (A few states are now attempting to change this policy so that adolescents who murder or commit a felony with a gun will be tried as adults.)

But the cruelest, most calculated, sadistic, humiliating, terrifying, and devastating crimes are committed by millions of people each and every year in ordinary homes on ordinary streets all across America. Rape, torture, and other violations of mind, body, and spirit occur every day *at home.*

Once in a while, a child will be killed by someone at home. Once in an even greater while, in order to survive, a child will kill someone at home.

Then . . . there is an uproar! It is only temporary. In no time at all, the "incident" will be forgotten and crime in American homes will continue unnoticed and unarrested. Who remembers little Lisa Steinberg in New York City?

So we as survivors grow into adulthood learning how to hurt, cheat, manipulate, torture, and how not to feel or value the lives, minds, bodies, and property of others. We also learn that the legal and social systems supposed to protect do not do their job. Finally, we learn how to recognize easy victims, because they look just like ourselves. Wherever we go, whatever we do, as survivors, the imprint of family violence always goes with us, shaping our perspectives and futures.

Criminal behavior is intricately tied to the drive for retribution, revenge, and getting even.

Alice Miller, psychoanalyst and author of *For Your Own Good,* writes that the victim of childhood trauma will tend to *endlessly reenact* the original event until he or she becomes able to bring it fully to consciousness, confront the pain of its memory, and then release it.[19] Criminals imitate and endlessly recreate, however unconsciously, the traumas of their childhoods. However, by identifying with the aggressor they reverse the roles and become perpetrators rather than victims.

Intervention once a crime has been committed, while perhaps necessary, is not nearly as effective as intervention *before* a crime is committed. But, once again, prevention appears to be a difficult concept for policy makers to grasp. It is my belief that this is so because many policy makers are also survivors of family violence who have never faced the abuses in their own histories, and so, in one form or another, they, just like criminals, are bound to repeat them.

Homelessness

The first time I ever saw homeless people was in Italy ten years after the end of the Second World War. I was sixteen years old. My family was on a European holiday over Christmas. I had just been given a fur coat.

The streets of Naples were patched with snow. Fires made of animal dung burned in the alleys.

As we arrived at a restaurant for lunch, a small crowd of people gathered to beg coins from us, the rich Americans. We passed them by.

They were still gathered after we'd eaten, so the adults in our group scattered coins before the small crowd and gave bread to the children, who grabbed for the warm pieces hungrily. It was then I noticed that many of the children were barefoot. I felt very embarrassed in my fur coat.

Throughout the rest of the trip, I kept seeing in my mind's eye those barefoot children and their families living in partially bombed out buildings or field huts made of straw.

Two years later, at the age of eighteen, I was on my own in New York City with $100 in my pocket and no job. A year or so after that, my sixteen-year-old brother came to live with me.

My first apartment, which I usually shared with a roommate, cost thirty-five dollars a month. I worked as a cashier in a restaurant for ten dollars a night and dinner. My brother worked in a bookstore stock room for forty dollars a week.

We moved to a one-room studio apartment with kitchen and bath in a renovated brownstone, where our rent increased to $125 a month. I lied about my salary to get the lease.

My roommate, my brother, and I all lived in the one room with two single beds. Whoever was the last to come home at night had to sleep on the floor. When my roommate was last, she took her pillow and slept in the bathtub. She and I split the rent between us because my brother needed his pay for food and bus fare.

Though we were dirt poor, we never believed we'd stay that way. Even so, we were all scared to death of being out on those streets, being homeless.

In those days, there was a bag lady who walked up and down Broadway with a shopping cart. She had wrapped herself from head to toe in white toilet paper and tied white plastic bags to her feet as shoes. The woman had a peculiar kind of dignity to her, but she scared the daylights out of me. I used to have nightmares about ending up just like her.

Since then, I've often thought about her, about how close my brother and I came time and time again in those early years to being like her, without a place to live, without real family, and unable to turn to social services. If it had not been for the *very* cheap housing available without references, we would not have made it. There were other tight squeezes for me later both in New York City and in Los Angeles, as well. Even with a full-time job, I often made a salary below the so-called "poverty level" of $3,000 a year in the early 1960s.

Years ago, people thought of the homeless as skid row addicts and alcoholics exclusively. Then, because of budget cutbacks, many mental patients were released from institutions without any follow-up care. Many of them ended up on the streets.

After the Viet Nam War, in the 1970s and 1980s, the ranks of the homeless were swelled by veterans who had returned home addicted to heroin or suffering from post-traumatic stress. They no longer could conform to maimstream society and no one offered them help. Now Gulf War veterans are joining the street population.

An estimated one to two million teenagers also are estimated homeless, living in condemned buildings, under freeways and bridges, and working as prostitutes or drug dealers.

But by far the fastest growing group among the homeless are families—two-parent families or women with children. The women often are victims of battering by their spouses or boyfriends.

In an economic downturn, family members lose jobs due to layoffs or companies moving or closing down. Lost jobs mean lost homes. No address often means no one will hire the prospective worker.

Today, an adult working full-time at minimum wage cannot afford the rent for one room in most American cities. Single women with children often work full-time without being able to earn enough money (first and last month's rent in advance plus moving expenses and deposits for utilities) to rent an apartment. Typically, their jobs are lower-paying and fathers refuse to pay them court-ordered child support. These women are left to choose between trying to get into a shelter (usually permitting only a one- or two-month maximum stay) or relinquishing their children to social services foster care.

If they choose the former, they must move from shelter to shelter month after month. Their children then are shuffled from school to school, unable to keep their friends, and forced to study in the chaotic shelter environment, and highly susceptible to illness, infections, and malnutrition. What chance do these children have for a hopeful future?

Survivors of family violence are particularly vulnerable to homelessness. Often, we don't know how a healthy home should look or feel or how people pull together to make a family, so the transition from sleeping in a closet, on a couch or back porch to sleeping on the street or in a shelter may not be as big for us as it would be for others. For many of us, *anywhere* would be better than the homes and abuse we came from.

Survivors suffer from chronic lack of self-esteem. We tend to engage in "magical" thinking ("Something or someone will rescue me at the last minute") and deny how bad things really are. We pretend that the worst case scenario could never happen. We daydream and fantasize about who we are, where we're headed, and how we'll get there, with no reference to everyday reality. Survivors often suffer from either post-traumatic stress or multiple personalities, conditions that make any crisis difficult to deal with realistically. Many experience immobilizing bouts of depression that make it difficult to take the actions necessary to preserve self and income before it's too late and we're out on the street.

In addition, survivors tend to trust either no one or the wrong people, wanting to go it alone or being too ashamed to ask for anyone's help. We tend to have a very poor sense of boundaries, so that money, property, and/or autonomy can be easily taken away. Not knowing who we are or where we stop and someone else begins enables unscrupulous, manipulative others to take advantage of us when we are feeling vulnerable or helpless.

Homelessness is the shadow side of our culture, the underbelly of its glitz and glamour. The growing problem of homelessness demands that we face what is wrong with our society, that we each take responsibility for learning how to interact without violence and for the good of all.

Unused buildings could be converted to minimum-cost housing for people working for minimum wages. Homeless people could be employed to convert and then run the new dwellings. People with extra space in their homes could rent a room to someone who might otherwise end up on the street due to loss of job or housing.

Tenants in large apartment projects could join forces and train some of themselves in child care, so that other mothers could go to work knowing their children are safe without having to pay as much as for outside child care services. Each mother could contribute food and toys to the facility. This would be a cooperative venture, a win/win situation providing meaningful employment for the women who stay at home, safety for the children, and peace of mind for the women who work outside.

Apartment projects could be cleaned up, organized for tenant self-government, and reclaimed from drug dealers. People can reclaim their lives and restructure their worlds if they empower themselves rather than allowing others to exert power over them.

But, survivors also can get very fierce when faced with impending disaster. Survivors are clever and resilient almost beyond comprehension. We have experienced so much pain, physical deprivation, loss, and abuse that given any glimmer of a chance, most survivors can succeed. Our efforts may not look very pretty or graceful or dignified, but then those criteria are absolutely superfluous under the circumstances. Survivors can cope with a staggering load of life's problems. That is why, if more and more of us face our histories and become healthy, we will be able to affect enormous changes in our world.

Intrapersonal
Behavior: Health

CHAPTER 6

Intrapersonal Behavior: Health

How to relate to and care for oneself in body, mind, and spirit is a great challenge for survivors.

Personal issues that are as yet unresolved and unconscious or those that are not acted out in society are internalized and enacted upon the intrapersonal state, in the physical, mental, emotional, or spiritual realms of one's own being. Of all the many survivor coping behaviors, the intrapersonal are the hardest for us to recognize and trace to a cause. It is my belief that they are also the most deeply ingrained and the most difficult to change. Even though these behaviors can seem self-destructive, we need to realize that they represent the final line of defense in self-preservation.

While western medical doctors and health practitioners are the professionals most likely to be consulted by the survivor about these behaviors, neither western medical doctors nor mental health workers are particularly skilled at treating survivors for the causes underlying these "symptoms." Often they dismiss him or her as a hypochondriac, as someone whose ailments are psychosomatic. Very often the survivor is given prescription medication to treat the symptoms without any attempt at understanding their origin.

Short-term, "quick fix" therapies are now also quite popular, as they give almost instant, if temporary, relief, often without drugs, and return people to work. Whether or not they can be considered "cures" is still open to debate.

Since few medical doctors have been trained to recognize the symptoms of childhood trauma in either children or adults, and since even fewer professionals understand that traumatic childhood experiences create long-term effects, the average survivor seeking help from the average practitioner is likely to run into a maze of difficulty. People in the helping professions need special training to deal appropriately with survivor issues and to spot correlations between past and present. Without that training, they may do more harm than good.

Because they are so vulnerable and predisposed to revictimization, survivors need to be very aware when seeking help, which is unfortunately a contradiction in terms. Chances are high that the survivor will encounter a practitioner who is also a survivor and who has not worked through his or her own survivor issues. Under such conditions, the re-abuse, sexual, physical, or emotional, of the survivor seeking treatment is not uncommon.

Since, as has been widely reported in the media, almost 40 million Americans do not have health insurance, many survivors will not have access to the helping professionals when they need them. And if no one cared for them, attended to their needs, taught them how to take care of themselves, or treated them as worthy of time, attention, and money when they were children, how will they know when to ask for help as adults?

Much major illness can be avoided by attention to diet, exercise, stress management, and relationships with others. But since survivors of family violence are usually involved with behaviors, either through addiction or other dysfunctions that compromise health, they are that much more vulnerable to illness.

Even with illness or chronic conditions, a patient can be restored substantially to health by consciously changing lifestyle and behavior patterns. But most patients are never told by their physicians how to do so and do not know to seek alternative sources of information. Most survivors are unwilling to give up their coping behaviors for something unknown, even if it is positive.

Instead, the patient relates to his or her physician as they would to a benevolent parent who will "take care of everything." The physician is rarely questioned or challenged, and the patient relinquishes responsibility for his or her own state of health. This parent/child interaction is encouraged by many physicians. Unfortunately, however, the patients most likely to accept such a relationship are survivors of abusive families all too prone to re-abuse by authority.

Every morning when I awaken, I say this simple affirmation: "I am responsible for the quality of my life." Sometimes there is nothing I can do about the external world, but my attitude, and how I use my energy can make all the difference in the quality of my every day.

The discussion of the behaviors that follow is an exploration of the delicate balance between life and death and the arena in which life and death interact, overlap, and battle with each other within an individual human being, the survivor of family violence.

It is also an exploration of the complexity of relationships between the physical body, the mind, the emotions, the spirit, the soul or lifeforce, and faith and hope or their absence. These intricate relationships constitute the innermost self.

It is at this core that the choice between life and death is decided. Many survivors find themselves unable to choose one or the other and end up living long periods of time in a kind of "half-world," half-alive and half-dead.

The behaviors described in this section evolve from that "half-world." By exploring their natures and evolution, perhaps we can achieve greater clarity as to how seemingly unrelated childhood experiences and adult behaviors are actually causes and effects in ourselves and in others.

Suicide

Probably all survivors think about suicide at one time or another. Some survivors think about suicide all the time. It is an enormous tribute to the courage of survivors that there are so many still alive.

If all other avenues for living in this world seem closed, suicide may be the only choice of action that a survivor feels free to make.

Suicide is a statement, the ultimate attention-getter, the final retribution. No matter how fed up the survivor may be with life, in contemplating suicide, there is at least some intention to punish others as well. If suicide is meant to relieve the survivor from misery, it is also meant to impart equal or greater misery to those left behind, if only as guilt.

Survivors fantasize about going to their own funerals. They also fantasize about going to the funerals of, or even murdering, those who hurt them so badly and caused their present desolation--especially if those people were parents or parent substitutes.

Suicide among teenagers is on the rise. In June 1990, a commission formed by the American Medical Association and the National Association of State School Boards of Education reported that 10% of teenage boys and 18% of teenage girls attempt to kill themselves at least once.

The suicide rate per 100,000 persons aged 15 to 24 was nearly 14% in 1990. For teenagers aged 15 to 19, the rate has tripled since 1960.

As many as 7.5 million children under the age of 18 years old suffer from some form of psychological illness.[1] According to *Time Magazine* in October 1990, the age at which children first exhibit such problems is dropping. "As many as 30% of infants 18 months old and younger are having difficulties ranging from emotional withdrawal to anxiety attacks."[2]

What lies behind these devastating statistics?

Disturbed relationships between parents and between parents and children have created a home environment that is hostile to healthy emotional development.

Instead of developing self-esteem, adequate skills for coping with life's challenges, achievable goals, and interpersonal alliances that nurture and sustain, these children develop Complex Survivor Syndrome, a variety of behaviors as defenses against neglect, abandonment, sexual exploitation, physical endangerment, alcoholism, and drug abuse.

Whether the parents' behavior is intentional, accidental, or the result of igno-rance, intolerance, or too many hours away from home and family, the result is the same: children who must numb themselves against the excruciating pain of not being loved and cared for by those upon whom they depend for survival.

We already know that at least two million children are abused every year. We also know that the perpetrators usually do not voluntarily stop their abusive behavior. What stops abusive behavior in most cases is for its victim to cease being available for victimization. Of course, there are many ways by which this can be accomplished, of which suicide is only one.

When I was fifteen, I tried to kill myself twice. At the time, I was virtually imprisoned in a girls' boarding school isolated on top of a mountain. The administration had orders from my mother that I should not receive mail, phone calls, visitors, or passes to leave campus. I was told that I would never see my brother again and that for the next year I would not leave that hilltop, no matter what the occasion.

Having been sadistically abused since the age of four, I felt at the time I had no more will to fight or to stay alive. No matter how hard I tried—I was an honor student, athlete, and student body officer—life was just never-ending punishment.

First I tried taking pills. That failed. Then I tried willing myself to die. I got into bed, I refused to eat or drink or open my eyes or speak to anyone and became catatonic. That failed, too, much to my chagrin, although I damn near starved to death after almost two weeks. No one called a doctor.

Soon after my suicide attempts, I began to get terrible migraine headaches. These continued to haunt me until I had the stroke some twenty-seven years later.

At seventeen, as a freshman in college, a friend gave me a little book on the theory of reincarnation. It fascinated me. For the first time an organizing principle for what I had previously perceived as a world of total chaos was explained. For the first time there was a purpose for my being born besides enduring unending pain.

As I understood the principle, we come into this life to learn specific lessons of our own choosing, and if we do not learn them in this lifetime, we will have come back in another to learn them later. I knew I did not want to repeat this journey ever again! Once was already more than I could handle.

Reading that book was the end of my active attempts at self-murder, but not the end of my more subtle self-murdering behaviors.

Many religions have teachings about suicide, most based on fear and punishment. Belief in them does deter some followers, although not all, from suicidal acts. Some religions encourage suicidal acts when offered to the deity, the ruler, or the state.

Survivors of violent physical and/or sexual abuse in childhood have experienced the fear of death. Many survivors, like myself, come to believe that their parents truly wanted them dead. Some survivors believe that their parents tried either to physically kill them in a fit of rage or systematically annihilate them with shame, neglect, or abandonment.

In either scenario, the message of death (as opposed to the messages of loving and life) came through loud and clear to the survivor of family violence. It is this message, whether received during infancy or later in childhood, that becomes a triggering mechanism for the various defensive behaviors comprising Complex Survivor Syndrome.

The messages of life say: "You are welcome into this world; you are valuable; you are a special, precious gift; you are loved."

The messages of death say: "You've ruined my life; I never should have had you; you are stupid, clumsy, fat, selfish, ugly; you never do anything right; you make me sick."

When, over years, a child hears mostly the messages of death from the lips of the most important, most influential adults in his or her world, those entrusted to give love and care, contemplation of suicide is only one small step in a continuing process, a step that could bring the process to a final halt, but not one that feels unusual or out of place.

Abused children face death threats every day, without defense, without recourse to outside help. With death threats day after day, month after month, year after year, the survivor develops a sense of living death far more painful than any real death could possibly be. Suicide, self-murder, becomes a natural and inevitable response to the constant death programming they've received from their parents by word and deed. Or it may be an act of self-kindness, a way of putting themselves out of their misery and a world seemingly out to destroy them. However unconsciously absorbed, death programming by parents is never ineffective.

Many survivors have developed a sense of futility as a by-product of their helplessness or lack of effectiveness in defending themselves as children against terrorizing behavior. For a little child in a violent family, neither "fight" nor "flight" is an available option. And when other adults all seem to condone or dismiss parents' abusive behaviors, the survivor feels totally alone. Under these circumstances as well, suicide may seem a very rational choice.

However, if the survivor does not commit suicide, that does not mean he or she has chosen life. Rather, it may mean a more subtle, more painful, more difficult to recognize way of self-murder has been chosen, one that may continue over a lifetime and depend on the development of a series of coping behaviors from the Survivor's Wheel.

If survivors believe their parents really wanted to see them dead, this death programming may go underground, becoming unconcious but not inactive. The body will obey and manifest the death programming from childhood, even if it is not consiously recognized. Therefore, it takes a mighty, conscious, spiritually assisted effort and the help and support of others to turn around this survivor pattern of self-murder. I couldn't do it alone and I don't know of anyone else who has been able to do it alone either. We need at least one witness to our truth. We need people who will support us while we grow and change, who will have faith with us that a different way to be in the world will work, and friends to provide some extra energy and strength when we slip or fall.

Choosing life is not a straight-line process. It takes as much undoing of past patterns as it does creation of present and future choices. It takes vigilance, as past patterns sneak up uninvited at times of dejection, exhaustion, illness, or loneliness.

Some survivors make the irreparable error of believing that their suicides will mean more to the ones they leave behind than their being alive. According to that way of thinking, not even one's death is one's own. What a terrible irony.

There are also drugs that can cause suicidal tendencies. The most recent and controversial is the prescription drug Prozac, which is an anti-depressant given to almost four million people. A percentage have had severe reactions that have led to murder and suicide.

However inadequate it may seem as a solution, suicide is the survivor's ultimate attempt to cope with unbearable pain and rage and to resolve the life or death dilemma he/she faces every day.

Unnecessary Surgery

What kind of surgery is unnecessary?

Unnecessary surgery falls into two major categories: "elective" surgery, voluntarily chosen by the patient for cosmetic purposes; and those surgeries recommended too quickly for the convenience of the doctor, before other, less radical options, have been tried.

Most institutions exist primarily to sustain themselves and only secondarily to perform the services described by their professional mandates. Hospitals and surgeons are no different. Hospitals receive most of their income from surgical cases. Surgeons receive most of their income from performing surgery, not from recommending less costly forms of health care treatment.

Research is revealing that a large number of non-essential surgeries are performed on survivors, particularly on female survivors. Women have almost twice the number of surgical procedures as men, almost all of them on reproductive organs.

Any number of surgical procedures can be classified as "unnecessary," depending on the underlying reasons for having them done and the patients' attitudes toward their desired outcome. Hundreds of thousands of caesarian section births are performed every year, many thousands of which are not required for the safety of mother or child. Instead, they are scheduled for the convenience of the physician, who, by setting a specific hour and date for the birth to occur, avoids having to be on call for days or weeks at a time. A caesarian section adds enormously to the cost of birthing a baby and to the discomfort of the mother. It is an unnatural birthing process and should only be suggested if circumstances in the women's pregnancy really warrant it.

Hysterectomies are second in volume to caesarian sections as operations frequently recommended to women. (See chart opposite.) Millions and millions of women have been told by their physicians to have this surgical procedure. Young women in their twenties and thirties have had hysterectomies prescribed for them as birth control measures. The only comparable operation for men would be castration, which our society does not permit, as it is perceived as "cruel and unusual *punishment*," even for criminal rapists.

With a full hysterectomy, all reproductive organs (womb, ovaries, fallopian tubes) are removed, creating artificial menopause. If hormones are not

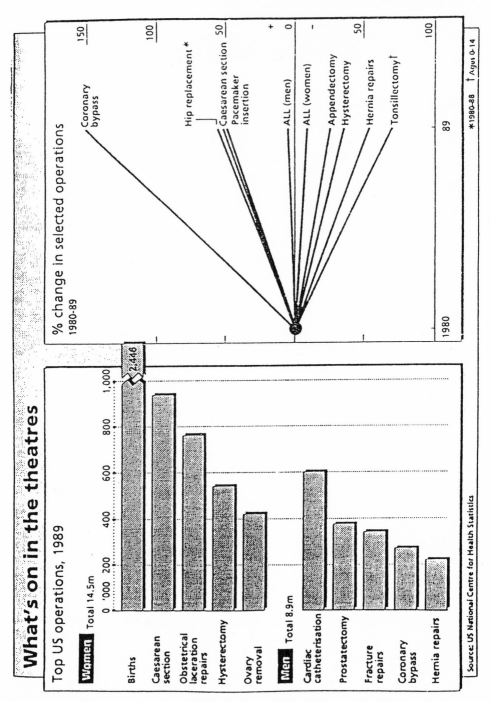

What's on in the theatres

Top US operations, 1989

Women Total 14.5m

Births
Caesarean section
Obstetrical laceration repairs
Hysterectomy
Ovary removal

Men Total 8.9m

Cardiac catheterisation
Prostatectomy
Fracture repairs
Coronary bypass
Hernia repairs

% change in selected operations
1980-89

Coronary bypass
Hip replacement *
Caesarean section
Pacemaker insertion
ALL (men)
ALL (women)
Appendectomy
Hysterectomy
Hernia repairs
Tonsillectomy †

*1980-88   † Ages 0-14

Source: US National Centre for Health Statistics

carefully prescribed along with the surgery, the woman will suffer considerable difficulties, including sudden and terribly stressful changes in physical, mental, and emotional stability. Some women not treated with hormones have suffered such trauma as a direct result of hysterectomy as to be hospitalized for mental illness. Other women have "gone off the deep end" and committed crimes, landing in jail.

Many men are circumcised as infants, which is certainly a trauma, although one they are told is beneficial for both health and religious reasons.

Some men have vasectomies as a method of birth control but apparently do not suffer hormonal changes as a result, so the trauma is not as severe as with hysterectomy.

All these operations when performed on survivors have increased dangers, for at least two reasons:

As already discussed, surgery may trigger memory flashbacks, which the survivor does not expect and is unprepared to handle. Also, as noted by Dr. Roland Summit, survivors of severe physical abuse and particularly of sexual abuse tend toward self-mutilation.[3] Self-hurting behavior can be overt (as with cigarette burns, razor blade cuts, etc.) or covert (as with surgical procedures). Covert self-hurting is harder to recognize.

Operations on reproductive organs (breasts, penis, vagina, womb, fallopian tubes) often are forms of covert self-hurting. The reproductive organs determine basic sexual identity and, at the most primitive level, a human being's self-image and self-worth. If in childhood they were the objects of incestuous activity, assault, and/or shaming, in adulthood they are probably the objects of self-doubt, self-hatred, and negative self-image. Getting rid of them, disguising them, or changing them may be seen by the survivor, however subconsciously, as a means of purging (purifying) horror and fear from his or her body.

Self-hurting in this way may also be an expression of the death programming survivors have internalized from parents' threatening their lives on a regular basis throughout childhood. If I was an object for brutal treatment by others when I was a child, if I was victimized rather than loved and valued, that's how I will treat myself as an adult, for that's all I know.

Self-mutilation with permission from the medical community can be subconscious retribution; but it can also be a reenactment of the original abuse, particularly if the patient is female and a survivor of father/daughter incest and the physician is male. The surgical procedure can be equated with being out of control and revictimized, while the surgical staff may be identified with the original abuser(s).

Self-mutilating surgery is revictimization on the most devastating and fundamental level, in that it takes away forever a significant manifestation of a person's physical identity. In performing such surgeries, a physician is most likely disregarding the overall well-being of the patient. As most of these operations are performed on women, one has to question whether or not some unconscious hostility towards women is being played out, not only by the individual physician, but by our society at large.

When survivors chose cosmetic surgery, it is frequently for the same motivations and with the same consequences as self-mutilating surgery. When I was in high school, many of my schoolmates altered their looks by having "nose jobs," or rhinoplasty, or by having their teeth straightened. Many of the girls (very few boys had cosmetic surgery then) went to the same doctor and ended up with almost exactly the same nose, no matter the shape of their faces. Certain styles of noses were popular then. The idea behind this surgery was simple: to visually fit oneself into a non-ethnic (in this case, non-Jewish) mainstream.

Hollywood has long been home to a coterie of plastic surgeons whose services have been used by stars from Milton Berle and Gary Cooper to Michael Jackson, Sylvester Stallone, and Elvis Presley and by vast numbers of women wanting to change their noses, jaws, eyes, and breasts to further their acting careers. Politicians, like David Duke, and politicians' wives, like Betty Ford and Nancy Reagan, have changed their appearance.

Cosmetic surgery can include face lifts, nose jobs, eye tucks, tummy tucks, breast reduction or augmentation, and scar recision.

In 1990, patients paid an average of $1,200 to $8,000 for facelifts, $1,200 to $8,500 for tummy tucks, $300 to $6,000 for rhinoplasty, and $1,000 to $5,500 for breast augmentations.[4]

Breast augmentation has been the most popular cosmetic surgery to date. Over two million women have received silicone implants in the last twenty years, almost 90,000 of them in 1990. More than 80% of the total of these operations were cosmetic, while only 20% were as a result of cancer surgery.[5]

Unfortunately, the FDA never tested the implants before they came on the market. Now the implants are being recalled, having already caused serious side effects, injuries, and lawsuits. According to Dr. Marc Lappe, professor of health policy and ethics at the University of Illinois College of Medicine in Chicago, silicone "has never been shown to be safe for long-term implantation." Dr. Lappe states further that use of these implants has "evolved with women as guinea pigs."[6]

Tests done in the 1980s indicated that silicone breast implants could trigger the immune system to make antibodies against silicone, which then would go on to attack the body's own tissue; but these results were not widely released or were ignored altogether.

Leakage of silicone into women's bodies has resulted in connective tissue diseases, tissue hardening, chronic fatigue, and lupus. For many women, the damage is permanent, since the implants can be difficult to remove.

Recently I came across an advertisement in a major daily newspaper for "phalloplasty"—penis enlargement. I could not find statistics relating to this procedure, but it is certainly being performed.

In the first major study on cosmetic surgery and sexual abuse, by Mary Froning, Ph.D., and Dr. Elizabeth Morgan, both of Washington, D.C., it was estimated that 30% of survivors of sexual abuse will seek cosmetic surgery as a way of dealing with their deep dissatisfaction with their own body image. Remembering that one in four women in this country is sexually abused before the age of eighteen, and that women represent almost half the entire population, the 30% figure represents hundreds of thousands of women.

Dr. Froning believes that many plastic surgeons are not aware that they are treating sexual abuse survivors, and the survivor may not yet have brought all memories of the abuse to full consciousness. This can be a dangerous situation for both survivor and physician. The survivor may have flashbacks or may act out the terrible memories, actually undoing the otherwise positive results of the surgery. In some of these cases, says the Froning/Morgan study, "the dilemma is that a sympathetic plastic surgeon may do excellent work but is perceived by the patient as an abuser." As a result, the physician's malpractice insurance and professional reputation in the community are made vulnerable. When physicians are also survivors (who may or may not have dealt with their own childhood trauma), interaction between patient/survivor and physician/survivor is liable to become very chaotic and emotionally difficult.

Dr. Roland Summit, head of Harbor/UCLA Medical Center's Community Consultation Service in Torrance, California, says that in seeking resolutions of past issues, sexual abuse survivors can be seductive, untrusting, fearful, manipulative, hypochondriacal, self-mutilating, depressed, suicidal, violent, untruthful, and obsessed by body perfection. "It's their way of taking back control of their bodies that was lost during childhood."[7]

The Froning/Morgan study cautions that no plastic surgery should be scheduled by survivors if they have not dealt with their anger toward those who abused them years ago.

This is a very good example of how Complex Survivor Syndrome works, as illustrated by the Survivor's Wheel. When a survivor has plastic surgery, three different behaviors, or spokes of the wheel (abusive parenting, unnecessary surgery, and anger) come into play and interact with each other over time.

Sexual abuse in childhood by parents or caretakers leads to self-hatred and a negative body image, which later prompts them to consider plastic surgery, not because of a real defect that is externally visible but because of an internal hatred. However, unless their anger (totally justifiable, in my opinion) against the original abuser is worked through *before* the surgery, the procedure which they hope will make them feel better about themselves is likely to have exactly the opposite effect. On the other hand, if they take the time to work through the anger and understand the grief, chances are that they may not choose to have the plastic surgery after all.

Hopefully, all unnecessary surgeries eventually will be re-evaluated by the medical community. Meanwhile, it is important to get information on the survivor process to both patients and physicians. Survivors must assume primary responsibility for informing themselves on all the ramifications of these operations, and not surrender their choices to "father figure" authorities. Also, the necessity of confronting childhood issues before agreeing to drastic surgical procedures that irrevocably change body form and function must be acknowledged.

Chronic Illness and Chronic Pain

On a speaking engagement, I met a woman who told me she suffered from migraine headaches. She was married and had several children but did not work because of the headaches. As she grew older, the nonprescription pain killers she was taking worked less and less effectively. Finally she asked her physician to prescribe stronger pain medicine.

Over the next several years, this woman became addicted to pain medicine. Her husband finally insisted that they go together to their family doctor and ask him to admit her to a drug rehabilitation facility.

In the course of withdrawal and the group sessions required as part of her treatment, she began first to have nightmares in her sleep and then, while fully awake and conscious, flashbacks of events in her childhood. Memories broke through a life-long barrier of chronic pain to return to her in her newly clean and sober state.

The memories were very painful, so painful that she had had to "forget" them entirely for over forty years. At ten years old, she had been raped by her older step-brother. She remembered seeing her mother looking down at her during the assault, but making no move to stop the boy or to help her daughter. The migraine headaches began shortly thereafter and continued until she was over fifty years old.

Only after she had processed her feelings about the rape and her mother not helping and protecting her did the migraine headaches become unnecessary as a survivor coping behavior, and then they went away.

Chronic illness and chronic pain are reminders of our mortality. They keep us constantly aware of our draining life forces. They dampen our willingness and ability to be alive, to accomplish, to be happy.

Very often people experience lower back pain when they embark on projects or ventures that frighten them. Lower back pain often relates to "not feeling supported" or feeling "out on a limb." Unwelcome people or situations are referred to as "pains in the neck" or "pains in the ass," phrases that may relate to physicalized stress reactions.

Stomach problems and indigestion can, of course, arise from what or how one eats, but they can also come from what one doesn't permit oneself to feel. This is particularly true in children who have strong responses to family dynamics but may not be allowed or able to express certain feelings, such as sadness, fear, anger, or shame. Not being able to "stomach" something or someone is a reaction to more than just food. A quick look at the shelves of remedies for indigestion in any supermarket will confirm how much we as a society cannot "stomach."

A dentist once told me that he had observed a correlation between childhood trauma and dental problems. Apparently, if a child is subjected to unusual stress or physical punishment while adult molars are forming (between six and ten years old), the efficiency of calcium production and utilization will be reduced, resulting in a reduction of exterior enamel formed on adult teeth--no matter how well the survivor eats as an adult or how carefully he or she attends to dental hygiene.

Louise Hay, in her best-selling book, *You Can Heal Your Life*, describes many physical symptoms and ailments and their emotional or psychological counterparts. She correlates pneumonia, for instance, to feeling desperate and tired of life, and having "emotional wounds that are not allowed to heal."[8] Pneumonia often follows the death of a loved one or other irreversible traumatic experience. Hay correlates arthritis to feeling unloved, criticized, and resentful.

Hay's belief is that body, mind, and spirit are interdependent aspects of the whole human being, and that no one aspect can be ignored or divorced from that whole without making its separation felt in some other way.

Abused children under verbal attack and physical and/or sexual assault or children subjected to violence in whatever form are able, by an act of will, to numb themselves to the physical experience of being in their bodies. They split off awareness of their bodies and identify only with their minds and spirits. As they mature, survivors of childhood abuse are likely to remain deaf and numb to the communications from their bodies and the physical world; they will miss or neglect important warning signs. Some survivors find themselves clumsy or accident-prone. For others, chronic pain and illness develop as the body's desperate attempts to have its needs recognized.

Like so many other survivors, I have had a large number of health problems, including migraine headaches from ages fourteen to forty; pneumonia twice; fallopian tumor, benign, at twenty-eight which developed gangrene because I didn't attend to it when it was first diagnosed; breast tumor, benign, at thirty-two; and massive stroke at forty-one.

Before I started to really heal myself and listen to the information my body was trying to give me, I could tolerate an almost unbelievable amount of pain. In the past, tolerating pain was necessary for my survival; and I didn't know any other way. Now I can tolerate almost no pain at all. Now, before I take even an aspirin, I make every effort to discover what is causing my pain, my discomfort, my dis-ease. For the last ten years, I have been able to stay quite well, for which I am extremely grateful.

It is frequently the case that those who suffer from chronic illness or chronic pain will at some point experience being regarded and treated by medical professionals as patients who are "making it up," whose symptoms are "psychosomatic." The original derivation of the term *psychosomatic* is from *psycho*, relating to the mind, and *soma*, relating to the body. It describes the interaction between mind and body. Because western culture tends to consider the mind as operating independently of the body, when a disease is described as "psychosomatic" or "all in your mind," the implication is that it is somehow less real than disease clearly traceable to a physical malfunction. There are those physicians who treat the body and those who treat the mind, the psyche, mental and emotional states, and the two realms are kept separate. But is this approach realistic?

In the early years of his clinical practice, Sigmund Freud, father of psychoanalysis, was sent a number of women suffering from the "psychosomatic" illness of hysteria (a term popular before the turn of this century to describe fainting, unexplained and temporary paralysis, hyperventilation, and other like symptoms without apparent physical cause). In working with eighteen of these women, Freud was amazed to find that all of them had been sexually abused in childhood or adolescence.

Freud wrote up and published his findings, but Victorian morality was at its height, and all hell broke loose. He was censured, ridiculed, and ostracized. One year later, Freud recanted his findings in favor of his theory of infantile sexuality, from which it could be concluded that all those women had simply invented the stories of their abuse. Freud thus cleared himself of censure, reinstated himself professionally, and effectively sanctioned abuse of women and children for another hundred years.

Of course, what was "invented" was Freud's "theory," not the revelations of his case studies. His "theory" has become part of the western mythology that still allows women and children to be dismissed, ignored, and denied fair hearings before the law when they reveal the horrors of their experiences of emotional, physical, and/or sexual abuse.

Chronic illness and pain may be the survivor's subconscious way of asking someone to validate the pain of the past when they themselves are unable to articulate or even remember what that is. Without conscious memory or permission to reveal the trauma or neglect they suffered as children, they are left with only the relentless illness or pain as traces. Chances are, with skillful encouragement to talk about underlying fears, griefs, and shame, the current pain or illness will become less necessary as coping behavior.

Reproduction

Survivors of childhood violence may have deep-seated feelings about whether or not to have children, feelings that have nothing to do with their financial status or relationship with spouse.

The birth of a new baby, an event that is filled with happiness for others, may be filled with fear and/or anger for survivors. These feelings may be accompanied by painful memories long buried, or even completely forgotten, of the survivor's own early childhood.

I myself did not feel capable of taking on the responsibility of raising a child because I had been abused, because I still had problems controlling my anger, and because my lifestyle as an actress offered no financial security. Fortunately, I have never regretted that decision. Fortunately, too, when the opportunity to raise my stepson later presented itself, my personal growth and ability to cope had advanced sufficiently to allow me to enjoy and respond constructively to that responsibility.

Many other survivors decide not to have children for the same reasons, or because they fear or are unwilling to make the commitment, or because they recognize their own lack of responsibility, instability of lifestyle, or problems with depression or addictions.

Many survivors have miscarriages or a series of other health problems with their reproductive systems. Men may be impotent or unable to ejaculate, have low sperm counts, or become celibate. Both men and women survivors may choose same-sex partners. Women may develop vaginal infections, tumors, or become frigid; they may suffer from PMS or menstrual cramps and not be able to carry a fetus to term; they also may become celibate. In general, the rate of surgeries is highest among women (see chart on page 131). Perhaps future research studies will draw clearer correlations between survivors of childhood abuse and family violence and the incidence of surgery, especially on reproductive organs and breasts.

On the other hand, there are thousands of survivors that do have babies. Some hope that by so doing they will have at least one thing in this world that really "belongs" to them. They want from their children the unconditional love they never got from their parents. Unfortunately, they are usually disappointed, because infants and young children are almost always in need of something. Others have children to prove that they have worth, that they can do something positive in a world in which they otherwise feel powerless. Often they have these babies when they are not much more than children themselves. Without prenatal care, without education about child care, without recovery from alcohol and drug addiction, neither these young parents nor their children have much hope for the future.

Some survivors of physical abuse are afraid to touch or handle their infants for fear they will do to their own children what was once done to them. No touching in infancy can mean death. A child who is rarely touched does not bond with its parents. Having never bonded, the child does not develop a sense of healthy boundaries and does not understand closeness or healthy separateness, i.e., what makes an individual. The resulting feelings of emptiness frequently lead to addictive behaviors.

If survivors have not, to some significant degree, worked out their anger, depression, addictions, and intimacy issues, they are going to have an extremely difficult time being parents to their children. In the process of parenting, old issues of control, violence, and abandonment inevitably will surface. Survivors never intend to hurt their own children, but they often do, if they have not dealt with their own childhood hurts and their impact on their adult lives.

Many survivors want to believe they can walk away from the past and leave it all behind, an attitude supported by our society. But we all, including survivors, carry our histories with us, and these histories play out in resurging memories, repeated behaviors, and relationships that duplicate childhood experiences with our parents. It is particularly in relationship with children that our pasts come alive once again.

Parents see themselves in their children. For survivors of family violence, this reflection can be very painful, evoking memories of scoldings, harsh and violent punishments, unkind words, loneliness, and terror of the parents from whom one longed to receive love and protection. These memories come flooding back, along with feelings of ambivalence, anger, outrage, depression, and grief. Survivors can find themselves at one moment doing to their children exactly what their parents did to them, and, at another, attempting to do exactly the opposite.

On February 2, 1994, a drug raid on a Chicago apartment revealed nineteen children, aged six months to fourteen years, living in two rooms and fighting with a dog for food left on the floor amidst cockroaches and feces. Whip marks and cigarette burns covered the children's bodies. All children were taken into protective custody. One child was immediately hospitalized and diagnosed with cerebral palsy. Three women and two men were arrested. A fourth woman, mother of several of the children, was in the hospital giving birth.

Reproduction can be read as either a cause or effect of survivor behaviors. Difficulty with reproduction is often an effect of a childhood of family violence and its negative impact on self-image and physical development. On the other hand, children born of irresponsible, unplanned, unwanted reproduction are at high risk of trauma, neglect, and abuse by their parents, and, consequently, of developing some or many of the coping behaviors on the Survivor's Wheel.

Anxiety, Panic, and Phobia

For me, the attacks of panic and phobia began with the publication of *Mommie Dearest* and ended three years later, when I had my stroke. I was particularly vulnerable when I was on the road making public appearances. At first, tranquilizers helped. Later, neither pills nor anything else would work until I could get home. Once home, the panic subsided, but agoraphobia took over and I didn't want to leave my four walls. Finally, I refused to go anywhere where I would be the primary focus. As the weeks went by, I felt more and more doomed.

No one seemed to know exactly what was wrong with me, which made me feel even worse. My behavior became a source of annoyance to other people, who thought I should be up and working. But I simply could not.

The agoraphobia was awful, but it was a definite means of coping with a far worse situation—that of being out in public and feeling totally unsafe. Agoraphobia impelled me to enclose myself in a tiny safe haven until the stress subsided and I could begin again to expand my zones of personal safety.

The survivor is remarkably clever when it comes to discovering ways to get through that which feels intolerable. However, our cleverness is often not in our own long-term best interests, if those interests include a healthy life.

Almost everyone has experienced anxiety, that uneasiness in the stomach along with a sense of indefinable dread, at one time or another. Anxiety may arise after making a mistake, or after an unsatisfactory encounter with someone, or about the outcome of some future event. Anxiety often relates to the fear that one lacks the strength to cope with what life has to offer. Anxiety can be experienced as early as infancy.

Certainly there are legitimate reasons for anxiety, such as the safety of a loved one, the illness of a child, friend, or spouse, or the results of a job interview or business strategy. But when the feeling of dread runs throughout the fabric of everyday life, when anxiety is felt to the exclusion of everything else, then, strangely enough, it becomes a coping behavior and takes its place in the Survivor's Wheel. It is then chronic anxiety, and it most likely has its roots in painful childhood experience.

Chronic anxiety is usually focused inward on oneself rather than outward on exterior events. Its source is lack of self, the sense that there is "not enough of me" to cope with what confronts me, that "I'm not strong enough, big enough, smart enough, etc. to handle this mess—and so I am doomed to failure if I try."

Anxiety is the cause of enormous discomfort for the survivor, as well as for those around him or her. It can take the form of constant chattering or worried withdrawal, compulsively going over the same details, taking unnecessary precautions against projected disastrous events, or compulsively eating, drinking, or taking pills to numb the feelings of fear.

The most common medical treatment for anxiety is the tranquilizer. Millions of prescriptions for tranquilizers are written every year without proper follow-up care. Millions of patients—often survivors—become addicted to tranquilizers. These pills sometimes are taken for years, sometimes decades, affecting the central nervous system and sometimes causing insomnia—for which the patient then seeks more medication. Some stronger drugs used to treat anxiety have more immediate and dramatic, direct and indirect side effects, such as severe depression, sometimes leading to suicide and murder.

Some survivors seek therapeutic help for problems with anxiety, but many become dissatisfied with the help they find, because so few therapists really know how to treat survivors of family violence. Over the years, I've heard hundreds of survivors say that their therapists never asked about the events of their childhood.

Often, though not always, chronic anxiety will build into a panic attack, an excruciating experience in which one may feel as though one is dying from a heart attack or suffocation, which, of course, only heightens the panic. Breathing becomes difficult, the heartbeat and pulse rate are elevated and may be irregular, palms sweat, the face is either flushed or ashen. The person feels an all-pervasive sense of disaster, doom, and death.

Panic attacks can be precipitated by real events, by flashbacks, by nightmares that seem real and relate to real past events, or by chronic anxiety and overwhelming stress.

Tranquilizers again are often prescribed and taken by patients who will do or take anything that holds the promise of preventing a recurrence of the panic.

Short-term cognitive therapy, in either individual or group counseling sessions, has been effective in treating the symptoms of panic attack. In eight or twelve sessions, cognitive therapy can teach the survivor how to handle the problem in a step-by-step way; but whether it is effective in preventing panic attacks over many years has yet to be proven.

Chronic anxiety, anxiety attacks, and the fear of recurring panic attacks can severely hamper a person's ability to participate in and contribute to society. Such internal stress can lead to the formation of phobias. A phobia is defined as "an obsessive or irrational fear or anxiety."[9] Manifestations of phobias are aversion, dread, and inability to perform a certain task or to be in certain places, such as high places or open spaces. Phobics can fear almost anything: driving alone, being in crowds, insects, animals, being dirty, being lost, etc.

Agoraphobia, or fear of open places, such as I experienced, can become so severe that the sufferer cannot leave the house, or one room in the house, or even his/her bed. Agoraphobia usually affects those who have already experienced panic attacks. It may start out as the fear of suffering a panic attack in a public place, such as at work, at a restaurant, or in the supermarket, and then generalize into not wanting to leave home. It used to be called the "housewife's disease," because it afflicts so many women, but statistics show that millions of people, both men and women, suffer from agoraphobia.

If a parent is suffering from any anxiety, panic, and/or phobia, chances are that they are so self-involved and frightened that they are not available to their children in any positive way. The children are left to fend for themselves, to meet their needs any way they can, and to sort out their fears and other feelings without support or assistance.

Agoraphobic parents do not attend school events for their children. They rarely participate in family outings or vacations. If the condition is severe enough, parental agoraphobia will affect a role reversal whereby the child is caring for the parent, preparing meals, cleaning the house, often lying to friends and family, and negotiating the world outside for the parent. A child is too young to do these things without paying a heavy price in stress and anxiety. In this situation, the child has no opportunity to develop his/her own set of healthy needs and wants with any expectation that they will be met, for no one is available to meet his/her needs, to recognize his/her wants, or to teach him/her how to achieve his/her goals.

As adults, these survivors become co-dependent caretakers and enablers, enmeshed in the identities of others, or "needless" loners. It is hard for them to pursue what they want or need, because they have learned in childhood that their desires are not important, their needs do not have value. They will have difficulty choosing a major in college, a career in adulthood, and a friend or partner or spouse who can take care of themselves. They may even have difficulty deciding what to wear or where to eat. The survivor doesn't know how to interact with others or what their "role" is in a relationship, particularly if it differs significantly from their role in their family of origin.

Agoraphobia evolves from a sense that there is no safe place in the world, that one has been totally abandoned, that there are no personal boundaries effectively keeping danger at bay. In contrast, claustrophobia—the fear of enclosed or narrow places—evolves from traumas of confinement in childhood. Those childhood experiences could include punishments such as being locked in attics, closets, or small spaces or being tied up, or being left in the crib for long periods of time as an infant, or feeling strangled or smothered by parental (often sexual) behavior from which one could not flee. In adult life, the claustrophobic may not be able to wear form-fitting clothing, buttoned collars, or neckties. They may be afraid of being "tied down" to a desk, or of getting "stuck" anywhere, or they may need to work outside or to be on the go at all times so that no one can track their whereabouts. In relationships, they may express the need for freedom or independence and flee when anyone becomes too intimate, even if they are in love and a willing participant in the coupling. Everyday life becomes a constant state of flight in one form or another.

For either the agoraphobic or the claustrophobic, the behaviors are not consciously chosen. They do not know why finding a small, safe place, or fleeing from any hint of confinement is so compelling; they just do it because if they don't, they feel they are risking doom and destruction. Nothing else matters until the extreme or anxiety or panic subsides. I know this from personal experience as well as from having seen it in countless others. As a child, I vowed that if I lived to adulthood, I would never be locked up again; but it took many decades of my life to achieve real freedom.

My heart goes out to survivors caught in the vicious cycles of anxiety, panic, and phobia—all escalating behaviors that tap into the original childhood experience of feeling annihilated by those parents, caretakers, teachers, relatives, and other trusted authorities who taught us that we were unloved, unwanted, burdensome, unattractive, inept, and worse.

Sleep Disorders

An estimated 70 million people in the United States get less sleep than they require each night, and 30 million more are insomniacs hardly sleeping at all, according to information from the American Sleep Disorder Association in Minnesota. That amounts to an astonishing 100 million Americans reported with sleep disorders.

The most common sleep disorders are insomnia (inability to go to sleep and stay asleep), night terrors (extreme nightmares), sleepwalking, and narcolepsy (attacks of deep sleep when the person is not in bed).

Sleepwalking and narcolepsy run in families and are thought to be caused by genetic factors. Narcolepsy affects about 250,000 people.

A number of other potentially harmful behaviors that are associated with distressed emotional and/or physical states occur during sleep. They include head banging, violent thrashing, loud snoring, breath holding, and teeth grinding.

While I have rarely had insomnia, I have experienced night terrors and nightmares from which I awoke soaked with perspiration, shaking, and frightened. For years I also ground my teeth during sleep. At one point, the grinding was so vigorous that I actually cracked a molar that then had to be removed.

Studies have found the two major causes of insomnia to be depression and anxiety. Depression and anxiety, although occurring in the nonsurvivor population as well, are so common among survivors as to be considered hallmarks of survivor behavior. Sleep disorders often originate in early childhood as the result of trauma, family instability, or troubled relationships. For survivors of family violence who have experienced trauma at night and during sleep, as well as during daylight and waking hours, sleep disorders are commonplace.

No one yet has figured out why we need sleep. We only know that if we do not get enough or enough of the right kind of sleep, we become irritable, disoriented, and less able to perform at full capacity.

Researchers distinguish the two major kinds of sleep as REM (rapid eye movement, or active sleep) and non-REM (non-rapid eye movement, or quiet sleep). REM sleep helps the brain to organize new information and is the time when dreaming occurs. Children spend much more time in REM sleep and in the deepest stage of non-REM sleep than adults do. Elderly people spend little or no time in deep, quiet sleep and often complain about geriatric insomnia.

The individual biological clock can be very easily upset, resulting in sleep disorders. Anyone who grew up with alcoholic parents remembers the nights of strange and ominous noises, the arguments, the beatings, the crash of things breaking, and then the deathly quiet when no one dared to breathe for fear it all would start all over again. Sexual abuse victims often experienced nights as the time of assault and greatest terror. Month after month, year after year, they were awakened from sleep to be molested, seduced, prostituted, and raped. As adults, many of these survivors still cannot sleep at night, or do so only with the help of medication. Many cannot sleep in the dark and need a light on all night to feel safe. Many are "night owls," working at night and sleeping during the day. Some prefer not to sleep in a bed, and so they sleep on the floor, on the couch, or in a chair.

Years ago, insomnia was treated with sleeping pills (which do not cure the disorder and are highly addictive) and antidepressants (which suppress REM sleep and so do not help night terrors, which occur during non-REM sleep). One only has to go into any drug store or supermarket to see the number of nonprescription sleep-helpers available to know that many people suffer trouble sleeping.

While it is understandable and healthy to want to sleep, even nonprescription drugs are easily addictive. When artificial measures are taken, they are probably only temporary stop-gaps. For true recovery from sleep disorders to take place, the cause(s) of the problem have to be explored, unless even more serious complications and health problems are acceptable consequences; for what is not dealt with today just changes form and comes back worse tomorrow. It does not disappear.

If insomnia becomes addiction to drugs, there are two serious health problems instead of one. And if some other substance such as alcohol is added to the picture, there is the added risk of accidental suicide.

In the last ten years, with increased knowledge as to how to treat people more effectively for sleep disorders, sleeping pill prescriptions have decreased 50 percent. But in 1975, there were only three accredited sleep disorder clinics, and today there are 150 clinics and 1,000 hospitals with treatment facilities. Clearly, proper treatment is not the same as prevention. For that, we must address the problem's causes directly.

Depression and Anger

Depression and anger are flip sides of the same coin. They are the behaviors most used by survivors to cope with their damaged lives. Where you see depression, you can assume anger lies buried beneath the despair, though it may not be obvious. Anger is always a companion to feelings of helplessness and hopelessness.

Some survivors experience more depression and others more anger. I seesawed from one to the other. As a young woman, I felt my choices limited to anger, depression, or insanity. I mostly chose depression, because I was determined not to lose control and risk being taken alive. I had been locked up too many times, in too many places, and I was deathly afraid of ever being locked up again.

When one is depressed, all seems hopeless and nothing seems worth doing. One sees oneself as valueless, doomed to failure. "Why continue living?" one asks.

Depression is a way of "numbing out." It shuts down all systems to the minimum levels for maintenance and tunes out as much "noise" or stimulus from the world as possible. Any further shutdown would result in catatonia.

During my teenage years and young adulthood, depression became my lifestyle, or, more accurately, my style of nonliving: it kept me from normal activity and creativity.

In my interactions with others, however, it was my anger that people most often felt and that caused many problems. My anger was always so close to the surface that it scared people away. Any misunderstanding or disagreement turned into an opportunity for me to explode, like a smoking gun or a boiling volcano. In retrospect, it is clear to me that, in my twenties and thirties, I lost a lot of opportunities and damaged many relationships with my out-of-control depression and anger.

Since then, I've had to learn many, many painful lessons. One of the most enlightening was that anger could be positive if I used it expeditiously to propel myself out of the immobilization caused by my depression. I also learned that when I actually could feel grief, sadness, loss, and fear, then my anger would subside naturally. I learned that beneath my depression lay my anger and rage, and beneath my anger lay profound grief.

Both were tied up in my feelings of shame and fear. I was ashamed because I seemed not to belong anywhere, because I'd been abandoned, because I'd failed to receive nurturing and kindness, and because I was afraid that if my anger (rage) ever really took over, I would kill myself or someone else; for I was well aware of anger's negative aspects. Anger could easily exceed control to become rage, and rage could become violence. Anger could be used as a justification for aggression and suppression. Anger could be used to control others and to keep them at arm's length.

In my early thirties, a friend recommended a doctor (gynecologist) to me. He furnished me with prescriptions for diet pills, which were actually small doses of amphetamine—"uppers." I thought at last I had found a way out of the depression.

I lost weight and was not depressed for the first time in fifteen years. Even though I knew those pills had to be addicting, I took them for nearly three years. I had a hell of a time giving up the habit. There were no Betty Ford clinics then, no Care Units. Sometime later, I discovered that the doctor had been an addict himself and that my "friend" had become a cocaine dealer.

Many survivors turn to drugs, prescription or street varieties, for relief from depression and anger—"uppers" for depression and "downers" for anger. But feelings, thoughts, and experiences all work their way through the physical body. If they are not dealt with upon first appearance, they will find other avenues of expression. Depression and anger can show up in the body as high blood pressure, digestive disorders, back pain, respiratory illnesses, stroke, heart attack, cancer, headaches, insomnia, rashes, etc.

In my mid-forties, I finally began to be able to handle my anger. I had to cry almost constantly for a year before the seething volcano within me began to subside. The injustice, the pain, the loss of childhood and of the opportunity to have my own family, the mistakes in judgment I'd made over the years, the shame, the fear—I had to feel it all.

Feeling those feelings hurt. I honestly couldn't remember one single decade of my entire life that had not been really awful. My childhood and teens had been filled with every imaginable abuse; my twenties and thirties had been riddled with health problems, addictions, and the constant battle to overcome the effects of my past, all while trying to earn a living; and in my early forties I just barely survived a stroke, only to struggle for four or five years to recover the use of my body and mind so I could establish some kind of normal life and begin to earn a living again. But I realized that my life as a survivor of family violence wasn't a whole lot different from the lives of millions and millions of others, both male and female. In earlier days, that realization would have made me angry and depressed!

Post Traumatic Stress
and Multiple Personality

Post traumatic stress (PTS) used to be called "shell shock." It is a condition that occurs as a response to the horrors of combat on the battlefield.

Statistics from the military indicate that fifty percent of PTS cases will develop during the first week of combat. By the fourth week of combat, 98 percent of the active troops will suffer the psychological injury called post-traumatic stress. The effects of PTS range from mild to severe. Immediate treatment followed by return to the unit as quickly as possible seems to be the course the military now prefers.

Most of our troops who fought the Viet Nam War were not treated for PTS overseas. I remember hearing Vice President Spiro Agnew boast that our veterans were "red-blooded Americans" who didn't need reorientation to civilian life. As a result, hundreds of thousands of Viet Nam vets were sent from jungle combat directly to their home towns, USA, without any treatment. Today, many years later, some still suffer tremendously, both physically and psychologically, from PTS.

Benjamin Colodzin, Ph.D., who has worked extensively with Viet Nam vets, in his book *Trauma and Survival* describes PTS as "a sane reaction to an insane situation." He adds that having "strong reactions to strong and ugly events doesn't mean you're crazy."[10] War is an extreme and ugly event to experience. So is family violence, which is why Dr. Ray Helfer's acronym W.A.R. (world of abnormal rearing, see p. 158) is so appropriate to the survivor's experience.

Dr. Colodzin suggests that PTS is "combat mode" behavior, but that behavior necessary for survival in war may become a hindrance in civilian life. A vet described his experience in this way: "There are reactions that sometimes go on inside of me—in my feelings, in my thoughts, my ways of acting—that have something to do with my combat reflexes. Sometimes I may react to situations happening now with a way of acting that is meant to be used in survival situations, even when what is happening now isn't a question of survival."[11]

This description also applies to the experience of the survivor of family violence, even when specific causal events are not totally remembered or cannot be verbalized because they occurred before the survivor developed language skills.

Dr. Colodzin lists fourteen symptoms of PTS. I have found that most of these symptoms also apply to survivors of family violence and so are components of Complex Survivor Syndrome. They include:

- Vigilance and scanning: watching out as if something dangerous were about to happen to you.

- Elevated startle response: being jumpy when something unexpected happens or when someone touches you from behind.

- Blunted affect or psychic numbing: reduction or loss of ability to feel and to be close to others, to experience happiness, love, creativity, playfulness, spontaneity.

- Aggressive, controlling behavior: acting with violence (physical, mental, emotional, and/or verbal). Willingness to use force to get your way, even when it is not a survival situation.

- Interruption of memory and concentration: difficulty concentrating and remembering under certain conditions that activate survivor stress.

- Depression: in PTS, the condition can reach an extreme and is marked by exhaustion, negative attitude, apathy.

- Generalized anxiety: tension in the body, such as muscle or stomach cramps, headaches, etc. Worried thoughts, such as the belief that someone is after you. Sustained feelings of fear, guilt, low self-esteem.

- Episodes of rage: not to be confused with ordinary anger, this is a violent outburst marked with real danger for all present. Often more likely to occur after use of drugs or alcohol.

- Substance abuse: self-soothing with drugs or alcohol (use of prescription drugs as directed not included). Many PTS survivors use no chemical substances and do not drink.

- Intrusive recall: probably the most significant indicator of the presence of PTS. Old, usually ugly, memories that come to consciousness without any warning. Happens both awake and asleep, in dreams. Night sweats often accompany intrusive recall in dreams. Waking up in combat-ready posture.

- Dissociative experiences: memory of a traumatic event so powerful that present reality fades into background and is perceived as less real than the memory. In this state, one might believe that one is back in the old situation and begin to act, talk, and feel in ways that helped one survive in the past.

- Insomnia: difficulty falling asleep or staying asleep. Brought on by fear of intrusive recall in nightmares and high levels of pain and anxiety.
- Suicidal ideation: thinking about and planning one's death.
- Survivor guilt: feeling guilty about being alive when so many others who were friends are not.[12] Dr. Colodzin says of combat veterans: "It is not the task of the survivor to 'readjust' and act as if the trauma didn't happen. The task is to figure out what happened and learn how you are going to live with it."[13]

His statement applies equally to adult survivors of childhood trauma and neglect; for they, too, evidence PTS behaviors, particularly when they begin to confront their early experiences, either in reemerging memories and/or by sharing what happened with someone else, such as a therapist.

It is likely that in the course of confronting and disclosing traumatic events of childhood, the survivor will experience additional trauma as family members deny the survivor's memories, deny their own behaviors, and/or begin to scapegoat the survivor for being the bearer of bad news. Under these circumstances, PTS behaviors are likely to increase, at least for a while.

Usually the coping behaviors of PTS develop in late adolescence or young adulthood, when there is already a foundation to the personality structure.

Multiple Personality, on the other hand, is a coping behavior developed in response to prolonged exposure to extreme trauma and/or abuse experienced during infancy and early childhood. In this case the entire developmental process of the human being is affected, from the beginning of consciousness, before a fundamental sense of self has been established.

Multiple Personality is the highly complex, ingenious effort of a young child to preserve life while under attack, when no physical escape is possible. Sexual abuse and life-threatening physical abuse beginning in infancy or early childhood and continuing over extended periods of time are usually at the root of the creation of multiple personalities. Sexual and physical abuse of babies and very young children are the only known causes of multiple personality.

In cases of multiple personality, physical beatings and various forms of torture and humiliation often accompany sexual abuse, either sequentially or simultaneously. Ritual abuse in such forms as burying children alive, locking them in small, dark places without food or water for hours or days, forcing them to witness or participate in adult sex, forcing them to witness or participate in the killing of animals or other children as "sacrifices," and forcing them to ingest feces or blood is now being reported with appalling frequency.

No defenseless creature can endure so much terror, horror, brutality, and pain, and repeated encounters with death and destruction without attempting some form of escape and flight to safety. With no possibility of physical escape, the defenseless little person, in order to cope, begins to "split off" the self that holds the memories of terror and abuse.

As the abuse continues over time, more parts of the self as separate personalities are split off to cope with life-endangering assaults at the hands of parents, other family members, or caretakers. Often many separate selves are created within one survivor. Each has its own name, habits, memories, and age related to when the particular event of abuse occurred that is being "split off." These qualities are "frozen" in time, not subject to normal growth and development and the influence of external events. One of the many extraordinary features of the creation of multiple personalities is that one personality may have allergies, immune reactions, and other health problems that the primary or "host" personality does not have.

Many Multiple Personality survivors do not know that they have such a severe problem until they reach their late teens or adulthood, when relationship problems begin to wreak havoc in their lives, or when they find themselves in a strange city or in bed with someone they do not recognize. Hours, sometimes days, slip through the cracks, wardrobes appear unaccountably, and people say things like "You weren't yourself," or, "Don't you remember that you called me in the middle of the night?"

Years ago, when movies like *Three Faces of Eve* and *Sybil* were made, Multiple Personality was believed to be an extremely rare occurrence. Treatment of Multiple Personality was not always very successful, relying heavily on drug therapy and lots of time in locked wards of mental hospitals. At last, new treatments are now being explored, based on the current recognition that development of Multiple Personality constitutes a complicated life support system for those who suffered life-threatening abuse during infancy and early childhood. These new treatments recognize the necessity of validating the horror of those early experiences in order for the survivor to heal; but Multiple Personality remains a difficult condition to treat therapeutically because the damage was wrought so early in the life and so deeply and has interrupted all normal developmental processes.

It is my personal belief that male and female survivors, while experiencing many of the same forms of physical and/or sexual abuse, may develop different coping behaviors according to sex. Females more often form multiple personalities, while males more often develop into serial killers, mass murderers, or fanatic leaders.

To put it another way, female survivors of sustained life-threatening sexual/ physical abuse tend to internalize the struggle for survival, and, consistent with the archetypal female process, "give birth" to multiple personalities. Male survivors of the same circumstances tend to externalize their struggle for survival by targeting enemies they will have to vanquish, by asserting power over others. These contrasting behaviors are in keeping with the social and cultural expectations and stereotypes of female and male roles: to contain within and to assert outward, respectively.

I personally know several perpetrators of sexual and/or physical abuse who have never been censured or prosecuted for the damage their behavior has caused. In fact, most perpetrators do not admit what they've done to their daughters or sons but live a great lie of innocence, free to abuse and torture again. I also know a number of survivors with Multiple Personality. Generally, whether they're aware of their condition or not, their lives are a series of illnesses, suicide attempts, chaotic relationships, lost jobs, addictions, and bouts with profound despair.

As for serial murderers, most authorities agree their number is on the rise and that they are sociopaths and psychopaths beyond rehabilitation.

In all these cases, there is a monstrous injustice, one that will not be righted until enough survivors regain their own lives to fight for and protect those of tomorrow's children.

These extreme survivor coping behaviors, which are difficult and in some instances impossible to reverse or rehabilitate, should serve as a powerful wake-up call for society to focus primarily on prevention of childhood trauma and family violence rather than waiting to intervene only after the damage has been done.

The Immune System

Not so many years ago, no one knew about the immune system that is apparently so essential to keeping people well. Today a new field of medical endeavor called psychoneuroimmunology recognizes and concerns itself with the interrelationships between the mind, the nervous system, and the immune system. Holistic medicine has always recognized these relationships, but western medicine has become so specialized as to neglect the integrity or wholeness of a life in favor of treating parts and symptoms.

In its early phases, western science took an unfortunate turn with the development of "dualistic" thinking. By this process, the physical body was taken to be separate from the mind, an object for the mind's study, like a machine. As a machine, the body could be studied by reductionist methods, by taking its pieces apart and studying them outside their relationship to the whole of the organism. This approach has resulted in medical researchers and practitioners treating patients' organs, body parts, and symptoms as if they had little or no relationship to each other or to the whole human being.

More recent years have brought a new understanding that many major diseases plaguing modern civilization (heart disease, high blood pressure, cancer, stroke) are directly related to stress and personal behavior. How a person lives his or her life, what they eat, what they do for recreation, how much they exercise, and what they think and feel about life and about themselves has everything to do with their state of health.

The immune system apparently has been designated the body's translator between thoughts and feelings and physical responses. Because this is such a new arena of scientific inquiry, rather than paraphrase key points in the research that are relevant to survivor coping behavior, I have chosen to quote what I think are crucial elements specifically in regard to survivors of family violence.

"The immune system is a constantly vigilant sentinel dedicated to maintaining the integrity of the individual between self and nonself and mediating between host and pathogen . . . It is an enormously complex system, generally considered to be a primary agency of defense determining health and disease."[14] However, "an infectious agent, alone, is usually not sufficient to cause disease, but rather, a magnitude of factors must be considered."[15] These other factors are biological processes, such as the interaction between immune and central nervous systems, and psychosocial influences, such as public health conditions.

"It is known that: a) psychosocial factors influence a wide range of physiological, hormonal, and biochemical responses; and b) psychological factors influence the natural history of many disease states."[16] In other words, "the relations of people to their society and to the people around them can influence the incidence, the prevalence, the course, and the mortality of disease."[17] "Perhaps reducing immunologic competence at a critical time may allow a mutant cell to thrive and grow,"[18] thereby creating the climate for disease.

The words used most often above in defining the complex of factors influencing health are "stress" and "life change." Publications abound relating stress to heart disease, high blood pressure, stroke, and psychological problems. Major causes of stress, such as moving, the change or loss of employment, divorce, and the death or loss of proximity of a loved one, are well known even as to their relative values of stressfulness.

But psychosocial factors are active in a far greater range of health disorders, including infectious mononucleosis, Epstein-Barr virus, streptococcal disease, respiratory disease, dental disease, and periodontal (gum) infection. Diabetes also has been related to psychosocial factors in studies done over a thirty-year period.[19]

Autoimmune diseases, in which the immune system fails to function healthily, include rheumatoid arthritis, thyroiditis, anemia, lupus, myasthenia gravis, and polymuostis. Autoimmunity also has been implicated in multiple sclerosis, Grave's disease, ulcerative colitis, and Addison's disease.

There is a hypothesis that "stress, its subjective equivalent, 'strain,' or emotional distress, may influence the function of the immunologic system via central nervous system and neuroendocrine mediation," and that "*personality traits may predispose [the patient] toward autoimmune disease* [author's italics]."[20] Such personality traits include immaturity, dependency, perfectionism, feeling inadequate, having few friends, having difficulty coping with one's environment, blocked expression of emotions, strong, inexpressible anger, oversensitivity to criticism and/or rejection, and a lack of interpersonal boundaries. People with such traits are also described as having a tendency to overcompensate for their vulnerabilities with an outward mask of independence, self-assurance, self-control, overwork, and over-reliance on others for guidance.

These traits are typical of survivors, even to the extent that some appear as spokes on the Survivor's Wheel; yet almost nowhere in the literature on immune system disorders is the childhood experience of the patient mentioned as a determining factor. Studies deal only with the just previous events or factors in the patient's psychosocial environment, and not with behaviors developed over years as defenses against repeated trauma and life-threatening situations.

Some research, however, suggests that disease may be the human being's "defense against regression (to a more helpless state) and personality disintegration."[21] In other words, disease actually may be the survivor's way of preventing something worse, such as total loss of control (i.e., nervous breakdown) or death, from happening. *Disease may help the survivors to stay alive.*

Obsessive-compulsive personality traits, including compulsive neatness, indecision, conscientiousness, worrying, rigid morality, conformity, difficulty expressing hostility, concern with appearances and others' opinions, and conflicts over dependency, have been associated with ulcerative colitis. Those patients studied who had this disorder all reported having had over-controlling mothers.

Researchers have also noted that first attacks of disease were most often *"preceded by unhappy events and long periods of sustained emotional strain [Author's italics]".*[22] All survivors of family violence, abuse, and neglect during childhood meet this criterion. It is no surprise that most survivors have multi-faceted and ongoing health issues in adulthood.

These same studies on autoimmune disease show that the emotions most often found in patients were chronic bitterness and resentment; the majority of patients suffering from various stages of autoimmune disease are female.[23] Because of the intricate interactions between the immune system and hormones, oral contraceptives, which alter a woman's hormonal balance, are suspected of being associated with an increased incidence of stroke, as well as with viral disease, hypertension, pleurisy, duodenal ulcer, Crohn's disease, ulcerative colitis, gall bladder disease, photosensitivity, herpes, purpura, and lupus.

A positive change in personal behavior and personal attitude has actually helped cure many, many people from serious illnesses. Many books have been written on this subject during the last ten years, yet many people still are not aware of the information available and continue to believe and behave in their old ways. This is yet another form of denial, of the notion that if one ignores the problem, it will go away by itself, without requiring any time, effort, or acknowledgement.

With the increased cost of health care, the growing number of people without insurance, and the increased stress of living in our urban society, paying attention to one's own personal health is of greater importance than ever before. For survivors, however, paying attention to our bodies has been a negative and hurtful experience, an experience filled with shame. Many survivors will work hard to make their bodies look beautiful on the outside, while staying totally dissociated from their inner condition, their feelings, emotions, and thoughts. They do not understand that, even while they hide from themselves, powerful messages are being sent to the immune system to regulate personal health.

Other survivors layer their bodies with fat, creating a protective shield to fend off intrusion from the outside world and other people. They hide behind this barrier, without which they are too afraid to function.

Today, with the AIDS disease devastating many communities, attention to a healthy immune system is vital. Once again, lifestyle choices and staying in touch with oneself can make a significant difference in one's state of health.

The idea that we ourselves are our own best healers is a powerful one. It does not permit being seduced by the promise of "quick fixes," nor does it allow the beliefs that we can treat our bodies any way we want and someone else will heal them or that whatever happens to others won't happen to us. The empowerment to heal requires being aware and present within ourselves, which is often a very difficult task for survivors. The more we are able to maintain this awareness, the more we are able to know what is going on in our own bodies. Our bodies have very good communication systems that will alert us in advance of serious problems, if we are is willing to listen to them. Pain is one form of communication; energy flow or its lack is another; happiness is another. There are many more, of course.

Yoga, bodywork, and meditation are useful tools for reconnecting positively with the body and releasing stress.

Western physicians have very little training in nutrition, and many Americans probably do not get enough vitamins because most of our food is highly processed. Western medicine, for the most part, has not been oriented toward prevention of disease. More often, physicians treat problems after they occur, and even then they are slow to suggest changes in personal behavior and diet as means to recover and perpetuate health. Medications alone are not enough to achieve and sustain health.

Survivors tend to have trouble questioning or challenging health care authorities, whether physicians, other health care workers, or commercial messages on T.V. And yet, to the degree that we are able to learn to trust our own feelings and our own bodies, to allow our memories, and to face the past so that it can be released from its hold in the present, our positive concern for our health and bodies will grow.

Conclusions
&
Recommendations

Conclusions & Recommendations

When *Mommie Dearest* was published in 1978, it broke the dam of denial that family violence as child abuse existed. It was the catalyst that awakened people to the seriousness of the problem. Before that time, talking openly about the abuse of parents toward children was taboo, particularly if it was the victimized child who spoke.

Then the task was to break through the barrier of social taboo and personal denial that the issue of family violence included so many and caused such pain.

Today, many years later, the task is even greater. We are aware of the problem. We know that family violence is creating chaos, but we still are reluctant to acknowledge the scope of the damage and we just don't know what to do about fixing it. Not much that is being done is working. Social service systems seem only to maintain the problem, prisons seem to make it worse. It's frustrating, and costly.

No Safe Place: The Legacy of Family Violence offers a new paradigm, a new way of looking at the problem, a fresh perspective. The Survivor's Wheel is an alternative, helping one focus at the maco level, seeing how the dynamics weave together, shifting, reconnecting, and changing over time. It presents an organizing principle with which to first see and then approach solving the problem differently.

Children do not create child abuse. That is the simple fact. Recognition of that truth means we now have to focus on the root of the problem from a new perspective.

The theme of this book, the central premise of this work is: when adults treat children with violence of any kind, they create long-term physical and psychological damage that will affect the child's capacity for normal development as well as predispose that child toward choosing the use of violence toward self and others.

Violence is learned behavior. Parents teach violence to their children by the way they speak to them, their physical behavior toward them, their attitude and caregiving skill, and their example when they interact with others.

Neither the resulting childhood trauma and neglect nor violent parental behavior is relegated to any one gender, social strata, or race. And, this learning pattern of violence and victimization is passed from one generation to the next, so that once activated, it grows exponentially, which is to say— out of control.

So, what do we do?

Using the guidelines for healing from family violence set out earlier in this work, we need to rename, reframe, and reclaim. The first task is to rename.

Children do not create child abuse nor do they cause family violence. It is imperative to address the real cause, which is the abusive behavior of the parent(s) or primary caregiver.

Second task is to reframe: The issue is not just the immediate violence, but rather the long-term effect of that violence through the initial process of child development and across the future life span of that person as they mature into adulthood. The violence sets up a continuum of predisposing factors that result in addictions, failed relationships, street violence, betrayal of public trust, and of course, more family violence.

Once the issue is reframed, it is easier to see that no one method of solving it, no one professional discipline, no one social or educational program will be adequate.

This problem should not be compartmentalized because it involves the whole person—not just one act of abuse or the part of their life or one relationship or one adult choice, but rather a mind set and lifestyle.

The keys to solving the issue are cooperation and responsibility. The focus must be on prevention rather than just intervention.

Since The Great Depression in the 1930s, we have looked toward government to solve more and more of our problems, with the result that we have taken less and less personal responsibility for ourselves, our communities, and our local problems.

In areas of national policy, health, education, and defense, the federal government is vitally important, but not instead of equally crucial citizen involvement.

In the meantime, professional and governmental turf wars have to be eliminated so that all available resources and personnel are working cooperatively and in multidisciplinary teams.

Communities, neighborhoods, and individual people need to begin to cooperate and take responsibility for the quality of their lives as well. The isolation of people from one another is unhealthy, costly, and inefficient. Family violence, street violence, and violent social policy are all connected by the original experience of childhood trauma and neglect.

The third step is to reclaim and there is a lot to reclaim. We need to reclaim childhood for all children so that they can grow and develop their potential in a healthy, safe, caring atmosphere that respects their mind, body, and spirit, and treat them as valuable human beings. We need to reclaim our family as a unit of love and responsibility. We need to reclaim the way in which we run large systems, and to do that, each of them has to be rethought. They need to function as units of prevention of family violence, not just to intervene after the damage has been done, lives have been ruined, and generations lost.

Prevention has been a hard concept for policy makers to grasp because the outcome, the long-term benefit has been murky. Today, we are fortunate to have some concrete proof, through new research, which shows conclusively, I think, that long-term damage does indeed result from family violence, which should make prevention programs more attractive.

In the area of addiction, basic research has recently been completed to substantiate the new paradigm and the alternative organizing principle contained in No Safe Place: The Legacy of Family Violence. Four years of research by Patrick J. Carnes, Ph.D., Director of the Sexual Addictions and Trauma Unit at Del Amo Hospital in Torrance, California, involving 1,000 recovering sex addicts revealed the following statistics:

- 81% of men and women studied were sexually abused as chidren;

- 72% were physically abused;

- 97% were emotionally abused;

- Less than 17% of the people studied had just one addiction, while most had a number of addictions;

- The more severely people were abused sexually and physically, the more addictions they developed;

- The more severely they were emotionally abused, the more likely they were to abuse children of the next generation.

The study concluded by observing that "All addictions and co-dependency were, in part, a solution to the traumas and stresses of child abuse." However, in the past, "We [tended] to minimize the role of child abuse (in addiction). We [saw] it as unrelated or coincidental." But "what we were able to see (through the study) was that child abuse was core to all the above (addictions)."[1]

This is precisely the premise in the Addictive Behavior section of the Survivor's Wheel. Addiction is the coping mechanism for dealing with the emptiness and pain, that residual damage left behind from years of experiencing childhood trauma and neglect in violent families.

So, in this study, childhood trauma experienced in family violence is seen as the underlying core of multiple future addictive behaviors, exactly as the Survivor's Wheel depicts.

It was exciting to discover this research because it was published three years after the Survivor's Wheel had been created graphically and now validates the addictive behaviors section beyond personal observation, field experience, or self reports.

At the other end of the research spectrum from the psychology of addictions is the recent longitudinal study conducted by the National Institute of Justice, as part of the U.S. Department of Justice. That study made available in 1992 asked two questions: "Does childhood abuse lead to adult criminal behavior?" "How likely is it that today's abused and neglected children will become tomorrow's violent offenders?"

To find the answer, a study group of 908 substantiated cases of childhood abuse or neglect processed by the courts in the Midwest between 1967 and 1971 were tracked over fifteen to twenty years. A control group of 667 children with no record of having been abused, and matched to the study group for sex, race, age, and socioeconomic status, was followed simultaneously. The study found that being abused as a child increased the likelihood of arrest:

- as a juvenile by 53%
- as an adult by 38%
- for violent crime by 38%[2]

"The cycle of violence suggests that a childhood history of physical abuse predisposes the survivor to violence in later years. Victims of neglect are also more likely to develop later criminal behavior as well."[3]

The answer is a resounding YES to both questions posed and exactly what the Survivor's Wheel would predict in sections on Interpersonal Relationships and Destructive Social Behavior.

Charles B. DeWitt, Director of the National Institute of Justice, says, "Family violence—particularly violence against children—is a critical priority for criminal justice officials, political leaders, and the public we serve."[4]

In her confirmation hearing for Attorney General, Janet Reno told the member of the Senate Judiciary Committee exactly where she stood on this issue:

"The reason I think domestic violence is so important is . . . that is where violence is starting in America . . . . The child who sees violence as a way of life in his or her home is going to turn to violence as just part and parcel of their life as they become a teenager."[5]

It is heartening to note the top law enforcement officer in the United States understands the issue of family violence, its long-term effects, and its pre-disposition to use violence against others.

In May, 1994, (as reported by Barbara Vobejda, *Washington Post National Weekly Edition*, page 37, May 9-15, 1994), the Carnegie Corporation, a New York-based foundation, issued a report called "Starting Points," which had been compiled by a task force of business, medical, and childhood experts. Many of the findings on the current status of America's youngest children (under three years old) are disturbing, and two issues are particularly startling:

- One-third of the victims of physical abuse are babies under the age of one year old;

- While substantial formation of brain cells occurs before birth, formation of the connections among those cells (synapses) takes place before one year of age.

The report says that, with this new information, scientists believe that a stressful social environment during the child's first three years of life can activate hormones that will negatively affect brain functions in the areas of learning and memory.

This evidence no longer permits us to assume that there is no harm done to infants and young children in an environment of family violence that constantly subjects them to stress and trauma, which in turn affect their brain functions for a *lifetime*!

Now, how do we make use of the information, enlightenment, and empathy to begin solving the massive, multi-generational problem?

First by reminding ourselves that family violence will not be solved overnight. There are no "quick fix" answers.

Second, by engaging professionals from all relevant disciplines to share information, to share supportiveness, and to brave the temporary chaos during the process of discarding the outmoded while creating child-centered, family focused, community-oriented cooperative programs.

The arenas of concern are not only children and family but also:

1. Education and Day Care

2. Treatment, health

3. Employment and housing

4. Law enforcement, incarceration

5. Media

Education and Day Care

School-based child care and development classes are needed for both boys and girls before high school, preferably by age thirteen, before any of the children become parents.

Community-based parenting classes should be required before marriage licenses and birth certificates are granted (as we now require education before driver's licenses are granted).

Informational public service commercials are needed on the long-term effect of family violence and where to go for help. These should be run in Spanish, English, and other languages by locale. These infomercials should be created as at least a year-long series of spots whose message builds over time. This is an ideal area of cooperation between advertising, the entertainment industry, and the federal government.

Adult education classes for high school diploma in regular neighborhood schools is needed during daytime for local parents who have dropped out of school.

Federal, state, and local governments can take the lead in providing day care for employees' children again as a cooperative venture with the private sector. It is an ideal area for training and employment for people coming off welfare, displaced homemakers, and older workers.

Cooperative day care centers should be put in lower-middle income neighborhoods. Mothers could share or rotate responsibility much like car-pooling. Salaries could be provided for women who can remain in the neighborhood or apartment building and care for children while others leave home to work.

Treatment —Health

Prevention is the most important treatment.

In 1992, only 60% of the families where abuse was confirmed received any kind of assistance (McCurdy and Daro, 1993). Even fewer received quality intervention.[6]

- Healthy Start model of prevention through home visits to high risk families with newborns, prenatal care and follow-up. Healthy Start, the Hawaiian model now reaching 52% of Hawaiian families with newborn infants, has substantially reduced family violence and is part of the recommendation of both the U.S. Advisory Board on Child Abuse and Neglect and the General Accounting Office.[7]

• Families First programs for keeping high risk children at home with intensive intervention, relatively short-term, on call social worker. Cost effective—$2,500 to $5,000 per family versus $3,000 to $100,000 per child for out of home placement. About 500,000 children are currently removed from their family.[8]

• Nurse practitioners and midwives need to be trained and made available in small neighborhood clinics to give primary health care on a cost-effective basis, freeing hospitals and physicians for more serious cases of injury or illness. Every person must have a greater sense of personal responsibility for staying well. To do so requires information and access to prevention measures such as immunization, birth control, and basic nutrition guidelines.

• Substance abuse clinics, neighborhood-based and privately operated. Local people trained to provide services. One of the most effective has been the Lincoln Clinic Program, located at Lincoln Hospital in the Bronx, New York, started by Michael Smith, M.D., who trains substance abuse clinicians from the community to perform acupuncture in drug and alcohol treatment settings. They treat over 3,000 patients a year with 60% drug-free results in approximately two months. This program has been successfully replicated numerous times. Dr. Smith, through the National Acupuncture Detoxification Association (NADA), trains organizations to set up similar community programs.[9]

Employment and Housing

The old job market has gone. But there are many new jobs to be created in fields of community policing, community health care (i.e., nurse practitioners and midwives), substance abuse treatment programs, elder care, day care, reforestation, environmental cleanup, and affordable housing, just to name a few.

Cooperative, community, or neighborhood-based groups of people working together on home centered employment projects are the wave of the future. The big corporations will no longer be major employers. Individuals need to think more along entrepreneurial/cooperative lines than looking to life-long employment with one or two companies. Personal initiative will be the key.

• Affordable Housing—This is one of the most critical areas in the entire spectrum of violence prevention. All over America, there are vacant buildings and empty rooms in private homes, but current regulations prevent using these existing facilities for affordable housing.

Why can't the warehouses, empty houses, and vacant factories be turned into dwellings for homeless people and families by organizing currently homeless people with skills to do most of the work in cooperation with local union supervision and/or building trades volunteers?

Habitat for Humanity founded by former President Jimmy Carter is a perfect example of cooperative housing projects in which the recipients of the finished housing must participate in its creation.

Tenant councils need to be organized for all low-income or project developments in order to clean-up and take back the safety of those buildings. There are many good examples already started but they need to be initiated in every existing welfare or low-income project. It is not acceptable for people in this country to have to live in filth and fear. Local governments need to cooperate to make sure structural repairs are made and tenants are taught responsibility for maintaining good order.

Law Enforcement —Incarceration

The United States incarcerates the highest number of people and still has the most violence of any industrialized nation. Something is wrong with our system. It needs to be rethought. It has been said that the only way to stop crime is to build more prisons. When it costs $21 billion a year to build prisons and maintain inmates,[10] I think the American people need to be given better choices.

Community policing is the most promising new addition of an old technique—putting officers on the street, walking neighborhood beats so that police are seen as a safety resource and conflict resolution mediator.

Childhood history of all arrested for crimes of violence should be mandatory. In short time, it will confirm the scope of the damage of family violence.

Training on issues of family violence should be mandatory for police, lawyers, judges, social services court personnel, and the medical professional.

When incarceration of first time, non-violent offenders is necessary, instead of going to prison they could be offered the choice of working off their time in a conservation corps, for which they could be quickly trained to do reforesting, waterway restoration, and maintaining national parks. Otherwise:

- First time offenders of non-violent crimes should be sent to special detention facilities (such as closed army bases). There they should receive drug and alcohol detoxification and counseling, literacy education, and job training, since all will be rapidly returned to society.
- Efforts should be made to separate out drug offenders (if they have not committed violent crimes) and incarcerate them separately, again in closed but existing military bases. There they should receive detoxification, group therapy, education, and job training. Existing prisons are inefficient for any but hard core criminals.

These two types of facilities should be made as self-sufficient and cost-effective as possible by using the work of the inmates in providing food through extensive vegetable gardens, poultry, and small livestock operations. Inmates should be trained to grow and cook the food, clean the facilities, make their own uniforms, and create their own newsletter. No smoking should be encouraged and smoking allowed only in designated areas. Literacy for every inmate before parole should be required.

- Existing high-security prisons should be used only for repeat offenders and those convicted of any violent crime. Once again, in addition to punishment, time in prison should be used to achieve literacy, job training, and understanding of childhood trauma. All prisons should be maintained drug free. The death penalty should be permitted for child killers, serial rapists who murder, those who commit acts of torture and murder, and those who kill law enforcement officers.

Media

According to a study released by the American Psychological Association, a child watching three hours of television a day sees 8,000 murders and 100,000 other acts of violence by the time he or she leaves elementary school.[11]

Along with violent films and rap music, the result, says George Gerbner, a media violence specialist at the University of Pennsylvania's Annenberg School of Communication, "is the child becomes 'desensitized' to violence and considers violence a kind of norm, not an unusual thing, but a fairly usual solution to all kinds of problems."[12]

All media (T.V., films, books, videos, music, etc.) are influential. They need to be engaged as part of the problem-solving program so that the influence they hold is used positively and they can still make money, which is their goal. Scapegoating or blaming the media for all social ills or being the cause of increased violence is not helpful. Rarely could they be considered the primary cause. Rather, in the arena of social violence, they are a powerful source of role modeling, reinforcing negative values originally learned by children in violent families.

———————

No Safe Place: The Legacy of Family Violence presents a national wake-up call: recognize the long-term effects of family violence as a serious threat to our entire society or face extinction of that society as we know it.

Family violence affects all of us in one way or another. Whether or not we are survivors of its nightmare or professionals responsible for public safety and well-being,we are all taxpayers who pay the bill for more prisons, higher health care and court costs, and social services, and we are all thus still recipients of its fearful outcome.

Because family violence affects each of us, we will all need to cooperate with one another to solve the problem. It requires: prevention efforts, rethinking system delivery policies, cooperative ventures, early child care education, empathy by and toward survivors, and above all, personal responsibility from everyone. It will take time and patience. It needs to start immediately.

It takes a whole community to raise a child. We have the information to create that community. Now all we need is the will to do it.

Notes

Introduction

[1] *Webster's Third New International Dictionary* (Massachusetts: G. & C. Merriam Co., 1966), p. 2554.

[2] Jill Smolowe, "Danger in the Safety Zone," *Time*, August 2, 1993, p. 29-32.

Chapter 1

[1] Christina Crawford, *Survivor* (New York: Donald I. Fine, 1988).

[2] Jill Smolowe, "Danger in the Safety Zone," *Time*, August 23, 1993, p. 32.

[3] Women in Washington Lunch, 1992, see also: "A Tough Cop on the Trail of Hope, "*Utne Reader*, March/April 1993, pp. 70-76.

Chapter 3

[1] Patrick J. Carnes, "Abused Children, Addicted Adults," ©, June 1993, pp. 76-81.

[2] Jacqui Banaszynski, "Ties That Blind," ©, February/March 1992, p. 34.

[3] Ira Chasnoff, M.D., *National Association for Perinatal Research and Education Report*, Chicago, IL, 1990. See also, Michael Durfee and Deanne Tilton-Durfee, "Interagency Intervention with Perinatal Substance Abuse," *Children Today*, July-August 1990.

[4] *Journal of the American Medical Association*, April 1991.

[5] *USA Today*, April 17, 1991.

[6] Jacqui Banaszynski, "Ties That Blind," *Modern Maturity*, February/March 1992, pp. 33.

[7] *USA Today*, December 19, 1991.

[8] *McNeil/Lehrer Report*, PBS, January 1991.

[9] Jill Smolowe, ". . . And Throw Away the Key," *Time*, February 7, 1993, p. 56.

[10] Randall Odem, M.D., Washington University School of Medicine, St. Louis, MO, *Journal of the American Medical Association*

[11] *Beyond Rhetoric: A New American Agenda for Children and Families*, Final Report of the National Commission on Children (Washington, D.C.: U.S. Government Printing Office, 1991).

[12] *President's Commission on Physical Fitness*, 1991.

[13] *Time*, May 3, 1993, p. 24.

[14] Associated Press, "FBI: More than Two Dozen Serial Killers," *The Spokesman Review*, February 23, 1992.

[15] Ibid.

[16] *Beyond Rhetoric: A New American Agenda for Children and Families*, Final Report of the National Commission on Children (Washington, D.C.: Library of Congress, 1991).

[17] *USA Today*, October 17, 1991.

[18] "Teenage Sex, After Magic," *U.S. News and World Report*, December 16, 1991, pp. 90-92.

[19] Ibid.

[20] Jon D. Hall, "A Boy and His Gun," *Time*, August 2, 1993, pp. 21-27.

[21] "Legalized State Gambling Contributes to Betting Addiction," *USA Today*, June 26, 1992, p. 12A.

[22] Interview with Juliet Schor by Eden Stone and Peggy Taylor, "The Overworked American," statistics excerpted from Juliet B. Schor, *The Overworked American: The Unexpected Decline of Leisure* (New York: Basic Books, 1991) as shown in New Age Journal, November/December 1991, pp. 34-36.

Chapter 4

[1] Mark Twain, *Pudd'nhead Wilson*, 1894.

[2] Mike Snider, "Solitude Unhealthy for Heart Patients," *USA Today*, January 22, 1992.

[3] "Does Loneliness Lead to Heart Disease?," Pritikin, Vol. 1, No. 9, July 1991, p. 1.

[4] House Select Committee on Children, Youth, and Families data listed in *USA Today*, July 13, 1991.

[5] Barbara Hayes, Ph.D., 1990.

[6] Ibid.

[7] *Child Abuse and Neglect: Critical First Steps in Response to a National Emergency*, U.S. Advisory Board on Child Abuse and Neglect, Department of Health and Human Services, August 1990.

[8] *Beyond Rhetoric: A New American Agenda for Children and Families*, Final Report of the National Commission on Children (Washington, D.C.: U.S. Government Printing Office, 1991).

[9] Ibid.

[10] Ibid.

[11] Ibid.

[12] Ibid.

[13] Linda L. Creighton, "Silent Saviors," *U.S. News and World Report*, December 16, 1991.

[14] The State of America's Children Yearbook 1994 (Washington, D.C.: Children's Defense Fund, 1994).

[15] Victor Fuchs, Stanford University, *Science*, January 3, 1992 (as reported in The Washington Post, January 3, 1992).

[16] Ibid.

[18] *Beyond Rhetoric: A New American Agenda for Children and Families*, Final Report of the National Commission on Children (Washington, D.C.: U.S. Government Printing Office, 1991).

[18] Michael J. Durfee, George A. Gellert, and Deanne Tilton-Durfee, "Origins and Clinical Relevance of Child Death Review Teams," *Journal of the American Medical Association*, June 17, 1992, p. 3173.

[19] Ray Helfer, "Childhood Comes First", modified from *Pediatrics Basics*, No. 10, February 1974 by Ray E. Helfer, M.D.

[20] "Rights of the Child," Convention on the Rights of the Child, United Nations, New York.

Chapter 5

[1] *The Random House College Dictionary* (New York: Random House, 1973), p. 60.

[2] Carl Gustov Jung, *The Theory of Psychoanalysis*, 1913.

[3] Michael Ignatieff, *Blood and Belonging: Journeys into the New Nationalism*, to be published by Farrar, Straus and Giroux. As quoted in *Harpers Magazine*, March 1994, p. 20.

[4] Southern Poverty Law Center report, 1991.

[5] U.S. Department of Housing and Urban Development Report of a 1991 survey conducted by the Urban Institute and Syracuse University. As reported in the Washington Post, August 30, 1991, p. 61.

[6] Ibid.

[7] Ibid.

[8] Urban League report, 1992, as reported in *USA Today*, January 22, 1992, p. 8A.

[9] U.S. Immigration and Naturalization Service data as reported in *USA Today*, August 8, 1991, p. 5A.

[10] Commission on African-American Males data as reported in *USA Today*.

[11] Donna Britt, "What about the Sisters?," *Washington Post*, February 2, 1992, p. F6.

[12] U.S. Department of Education study entitled, "Women of Thirty-something: Paradoxes of Attainment," as reported in the *Washington Post*, September 1, 1991.

[13] American Management Association survey of 524 companies as reported in *USA Today*.

[14] Michael Ignatieff, op cit., p. 19.

[15] Lynette Lamb, "Kids in the Cuckoo's Nest," *Utne Reader*, March/April 1992, pp. 38-40.

[16] F.B.I. Uniform Crime Statistics as reported in *USA Today*, August 5, 1991.

[17] Cathy Spatz Widom, "The Cycle of Violence," *National Institute of Justice Research in Brief*, October 1992.

[18] Jill Smolowe, "And Throw Away the Key," *Time*, February 7, 1994, p. 55.

[19] Alice Miller, *For Your Own Good: Hidden Cruelty in Child-Rearing and the Roots of Violence* (New York: Farrar, Straus, Giroux, 1983).

Chapter 6

[1] Anastasia Toufexis, "Struggling for Sanity," *Time* Magazine, October 8, 1990, p. 47.

[2] Ibid.

[3] *Changes Magazine*, February 1991.

[4] "On the Cutting Edge," *People Magazine*, August 27, 1992, p. 61.

[5] Doug Podolsky, "A Ban on Silicone," *U.S. News & World Report*, January 20, 1992, p. 61.

[6] "Breast Implants--How Hazardous?," *People Magazine*, August 27, 1992, p. 63.

[7] *Changes Magazine*, February 1991.

[8] Louise L. Hay, *You Can Heal Your Life* (Santa Monica, CA: Hay House, 1984), p. 179.

[9] *The Random House College Dictionary*, 1973, p. 998.

[10] Benjamin Colodzin, *How to Survive Trauma: A Program for War Veterans and Survivors of Rape, Assault, Abuse or Environmental Disasters* (Barrytown, NY: Station Hill Press, 1992), p. xii.

[11] Ibid.

[12] Ibid.

[13] Ibid.

[14] Robert Adler (ed.), "Psychoneuroimmunology", *Behavior Medicine Series* (New York: Harcourt, Brace Jovanovich), p. xxi.

[15] Ibid, p. 5.

[16] Ibid.

[17] Ibid., p. 8.

[18] Ibid., p. 160.

[19] Ibid.

[20] Ibid.

21 Ibid., p. 163.
22 Ibid., p. 178.
23 Ibid., p. 355.

Conclusions

1 Patrick J. Carnes, Ph.D., "Abused Children Addicted Adults," *Changes Magazine*, June 1993, pp. 76-81.

2 Cathy Spatz Widom, "The Cycle of Violence," *National Institute of Justice Research in Brief*, October 1992.

3 Ibid.

4 Ibid.

5 Janet Reno, Confirmation Hearing before the Senate Judiciary Committee, March 9, 1993.

6 "Special Issue Home Visitation and Preventing Child Abuse", *APSAC Advisor*, Vol. 6, No. 4, Winter 1993.

7 Ibid.

8 "Keeping Families Together, Facts on Family Preservation," The Edna McConnell Clark Foundation, New York, 1992.

9 Michael D. Smith, M.D., Lincoln Hospital Substance Abuse Division, 349 E. 140th Street, Bronx, NY 10454, (718) 993-3100; National Acupuncture Detoxification Association (NADA), 3115 Broadway #51, New York, NY 10027.

10 Jill Smolowe, ". . . And Throw Away the Key," *Time*, February 7, 1994.

11 Kathleen Donnelly, "Violence—Part of American Culture," *The Sunday Capital*, May 17, 1992.

12 Ibid.

Bibliography

Adler, Robert (ed.). *Psychoneuroimmunology*. Behavior Medicine Series. New York: Harcourt Brace Jovanovich.

Berends, Polly Berrien. *Whole Child/Whole Parent*. Rev. Ed. New York: Harper & Row Publishers, 1983.

Bridges, William. *Transitions: Making Sense of Life's Changes*. Reading, MA: Addison-Wesley Publishing Company, 1980.

Carnes, Patrick J. "Abused Children, Addicted Adults," *Changes*, June 1993, pp. 76-81.

Colodzin, Benjamin. *How to Survive Trauma: A Program for War Veterans & Survivors of Rape, Assault, Abuse or Environmental Disasters*. Barrytown, NY: Station Hill Press, 1993.

Crawford, Christina. "Call It Terrorism at Home," *Changes*, February 1991, pp. 35, 74-75.

____. *Mommie Dearest*. New York: William Morrow, 1978.

____. *Survivor*. New York: Donald I. Fine, 1988.

Garbarino, James, and Gilliam, Gwen. *Understanding Abused Families* Lexington, MA: D.C. Heath and Company, 1980.

Garbarino, James; Guttman, Edna; and Seeley, Janis Wilson. *The Psychologically Battered Child: Strategies for Identification, Assessment, and Intervention*. San Francisco: Jossey-Bass Publishers, 1986.

Gelman, David. "Finding the Hidden Freud," *Newsweek*. November 30, 1981, pp. 64-70.

Hay, Louise L. *You Can Heal Your Life*. Santa Monica, CA: Hay House, 1984.

Helfer, Ray E. *Childhood Comes First: A Crash Course in Childhood for Adults*. 2nd Edition. East Lansing, MI: Ray E. Helfer, 1984.

Ignatieff, Michael. *Blood and Belonging: Journeys into the New Nationalism*. New York: Farrar, Straus, and Giroux, forthcoming. As excerpted in "A Cosmopolitan among the True Believers," *Harper's Magazine*. March 1994, pp. 17-21.

Fordham Institute for Innovation in Social Policy, Fordham University Graduate Center. *Index of Social Health 1992: Monitoring the Social Well-Being of the Nation*, Special Section: "The Social Health of America's Children," Tarrytown, NY, 1992.

Mellody, Pia. *Facing Codependence: What It Is, Where It Comes From, How It Sabotages Our Lives*. San Francisco: Harper & Row Publishers, 1989.

Miller, Alice. *For Your Own Good: Hidden Cruelty in Child Rearing and the Roots of Violence.* New York: Farrar, Straus, and Giroux, 1985.

____. *Thou Shalt Not Be Aware: Society's Betrayal of the Child.* New York: Farrar, Straus, and Giroux, 1984.

National Commission on Children, *Beyond Rhetoric: A New American Agenda for Children and Families.* Final Report. Washington, D.C.: U.S. Government Printing Office, 1991.

Smolowe, Jill. "And Throw Away the Key," *Time Magazine,* February 7, 1994, pp. 54-59.

____. "Danger in the Safety Net," *Time Magazine,* August 23, 1993, pp. 29-32.

Children's Defense Fund. *The State of America's Children Yearbook 1994* Washington, D.C.: , 1994.

U.S. Advisory Board on Child Abuse and Neglect. *Child Abuse and Neglect: Critical First Steps in Response to a National Emergency.* Washington, D.C.: U.S. Department of Health and Human Services, August 1990.

Vanderbilt, Heidi. "Incest: A Chilling Report," *Lear's,* February 1992, pp. 49-77.

Walker, Lenore E. *Terrifying Love: Why Battered Women Kill and How Society Responds.* New York: Harper Perennial, 1989.

Widom, Cathy Spatz. "The Cycle of Violence," *National Institute of Justice Research in Brief,* October 1992.

About the Author

Christina Crawford is an internationally recognized, best-selling author. She is an advocate for the rights of women and children, a pioneer in making child abuse an issue of national concern, a communicator about the long-term effects of childhood trauma on adult survivors, a business-woman, writer-producer, public speaker, and workshop presenter. She was Commissioner for Children's Services in the County of Los Angeles and earned her Masters Degree in Communication Management from the University of Southern California. Her autobiographical first book, *Mommie Dearest*, was on *The New York Times* bestseller list for 42 weeks, and was later made into a film by Paramount. Her second book, *Black Widow*, was also a bestseller, and has been translated in seven languages. Her third book, *Survivor*, was published in 1988. She currently lives in northern Idaho and can be contacted at the following address:

HCR 1, Box 310
Tensed, Idaho 83870